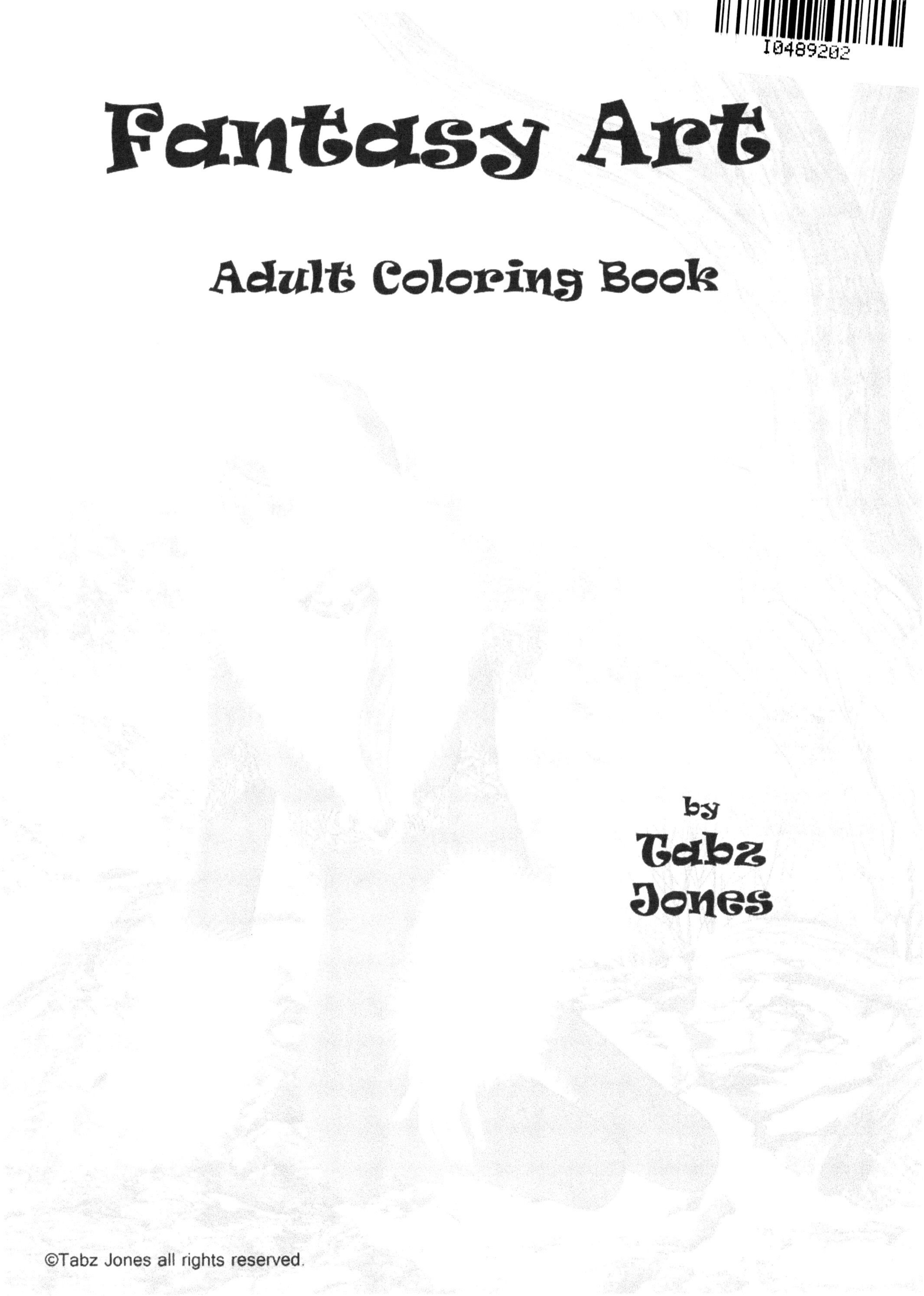

Fantasy Art

Adult Coloring Book

by
Tabz
Jones

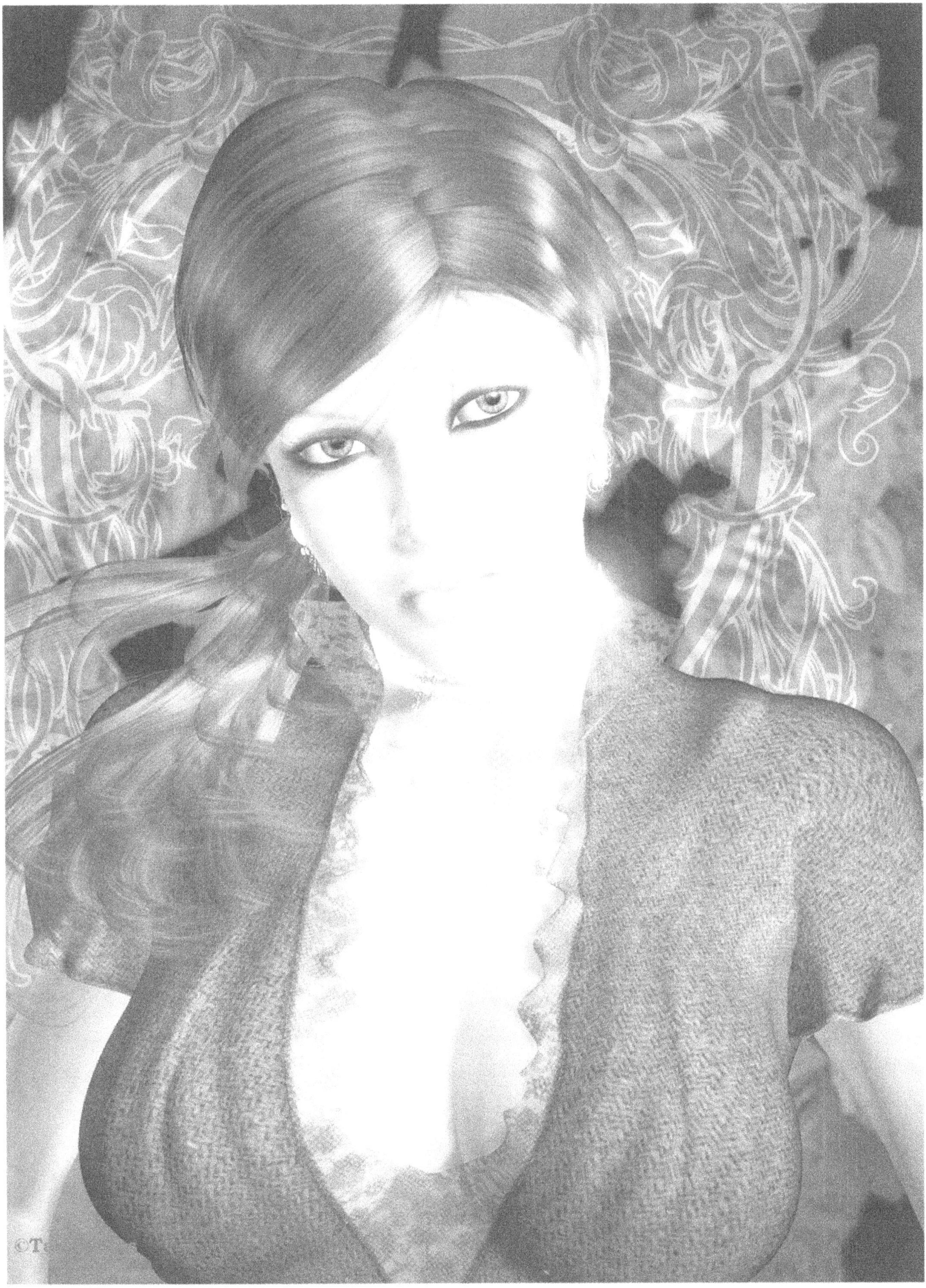

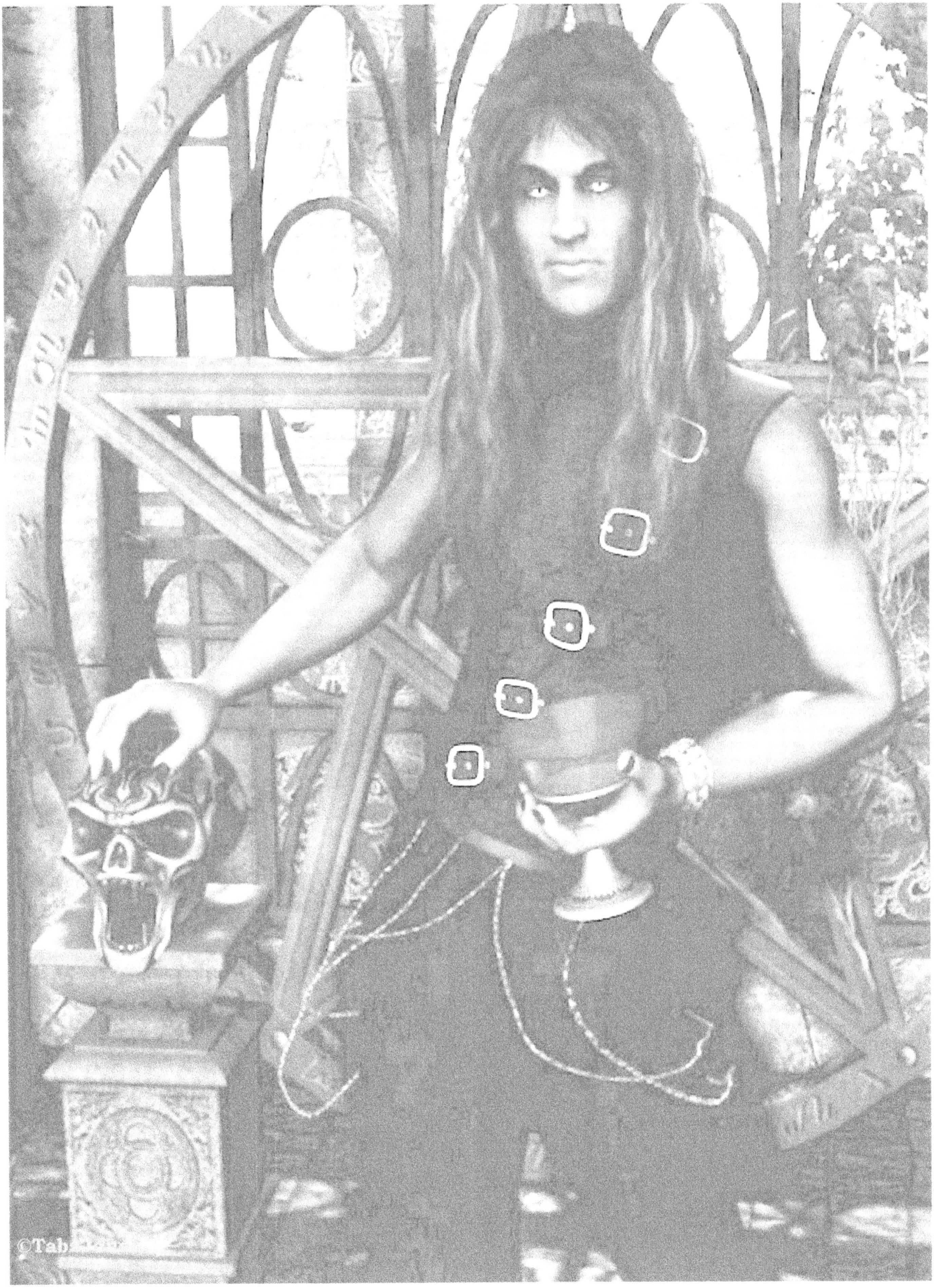
©Tab

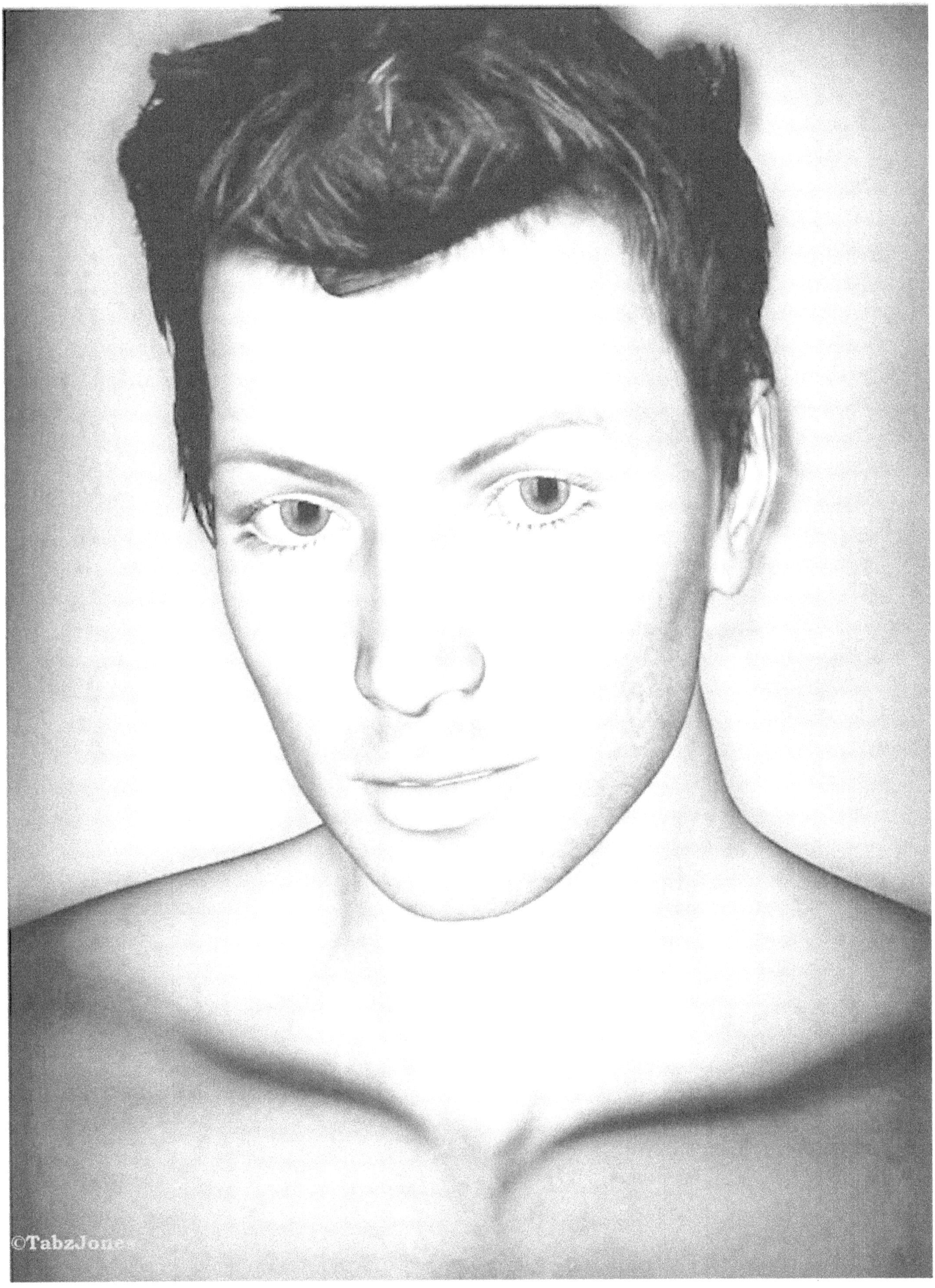
©TabzJones

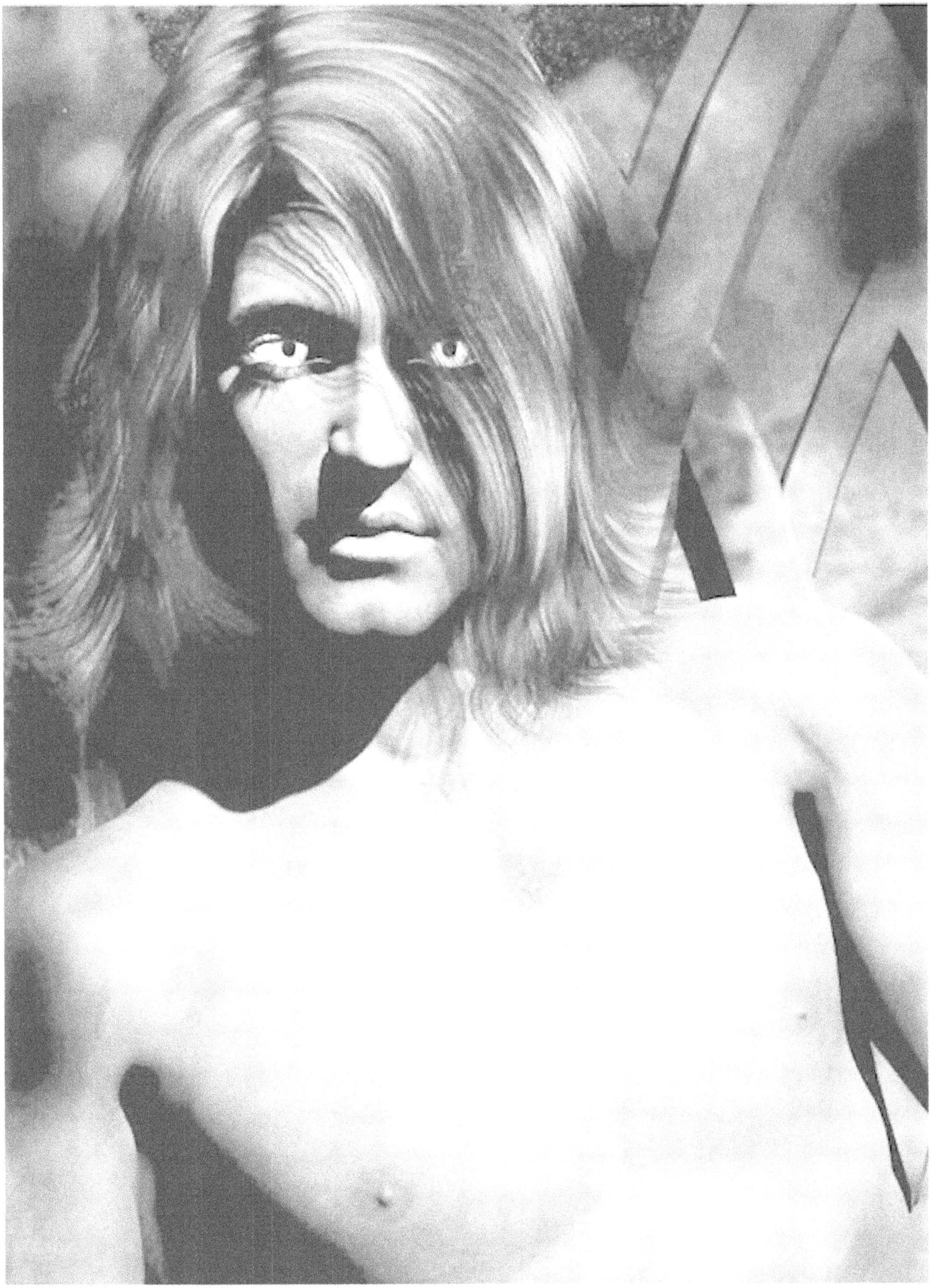

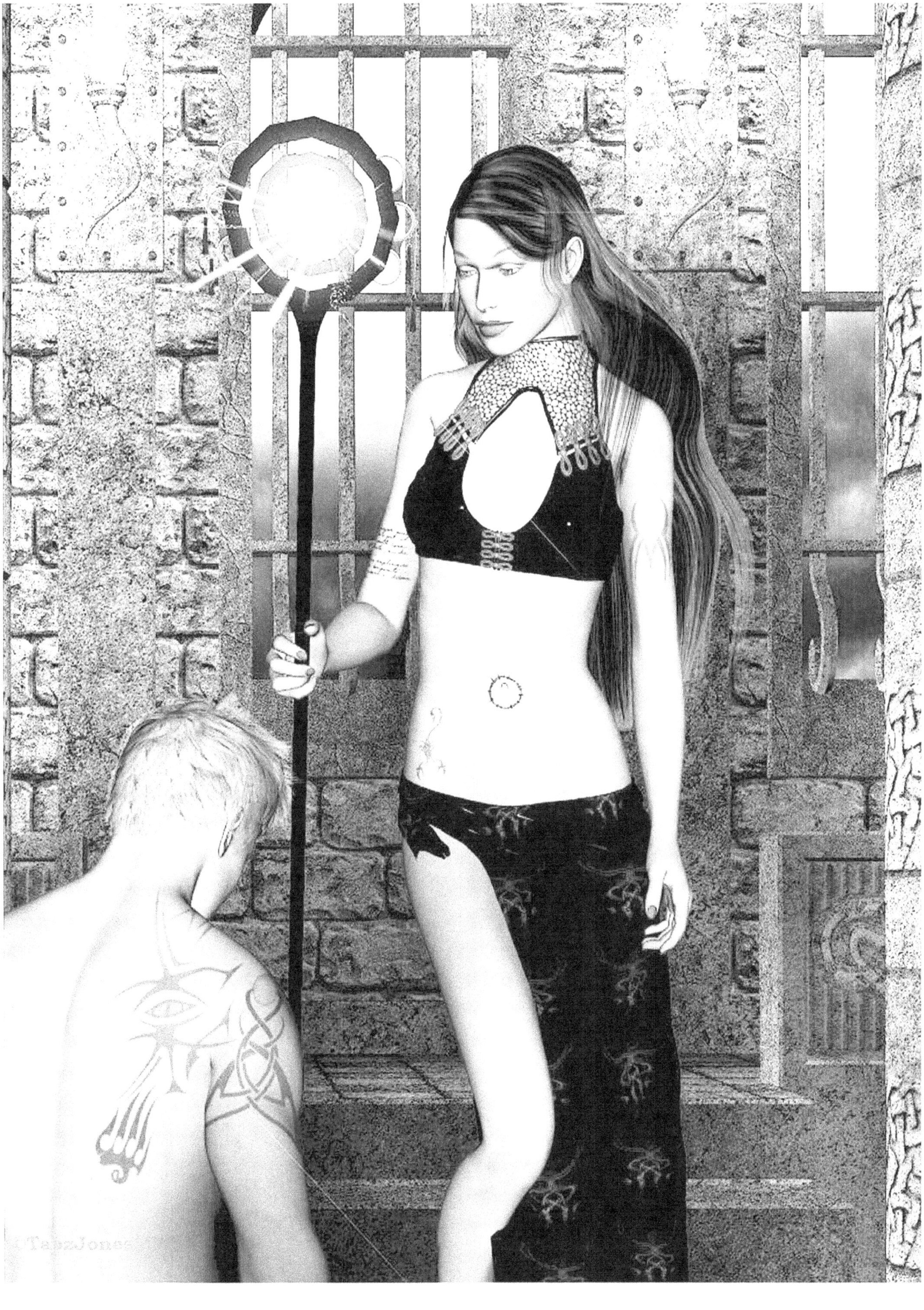
TabzJones

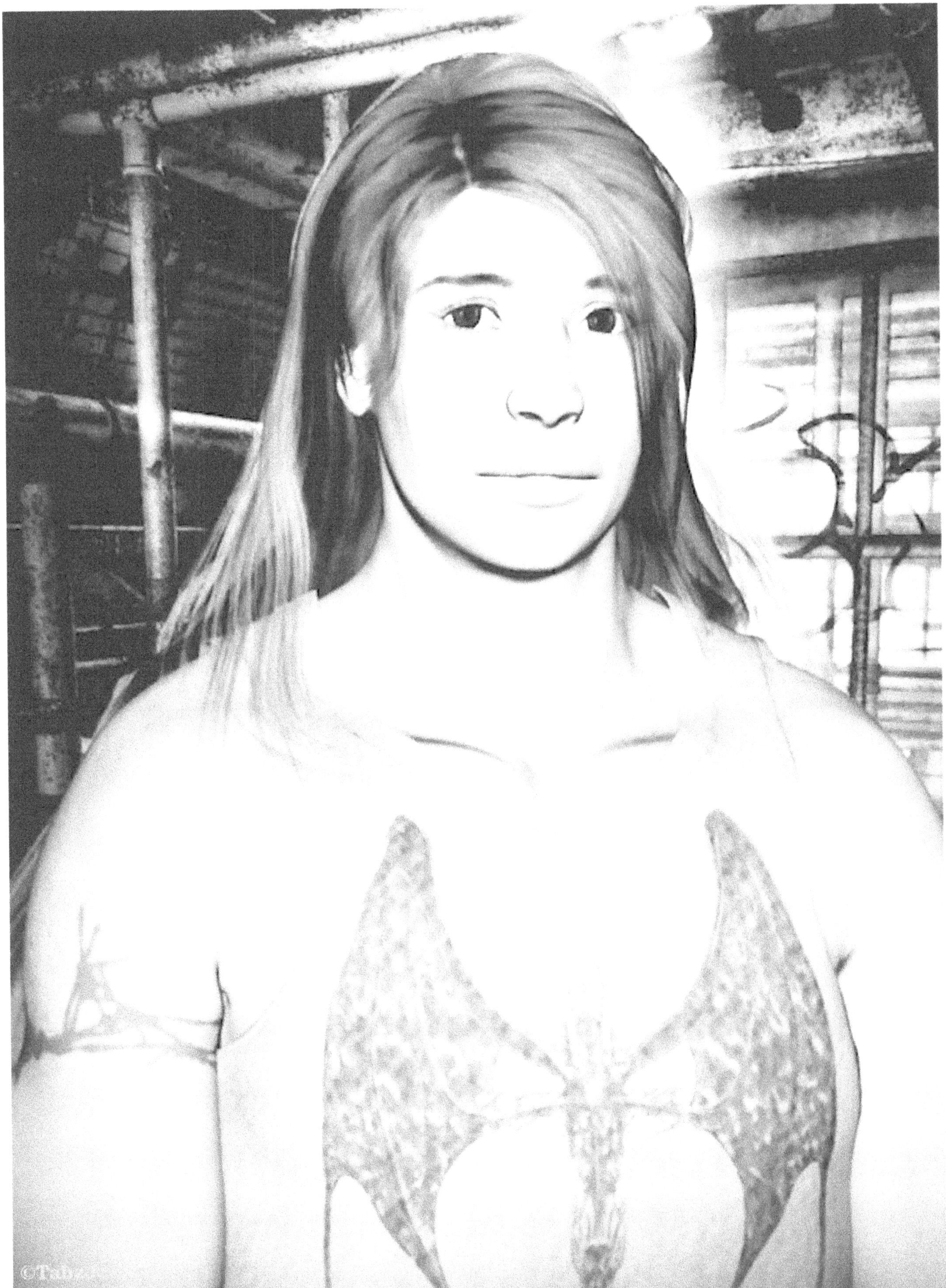

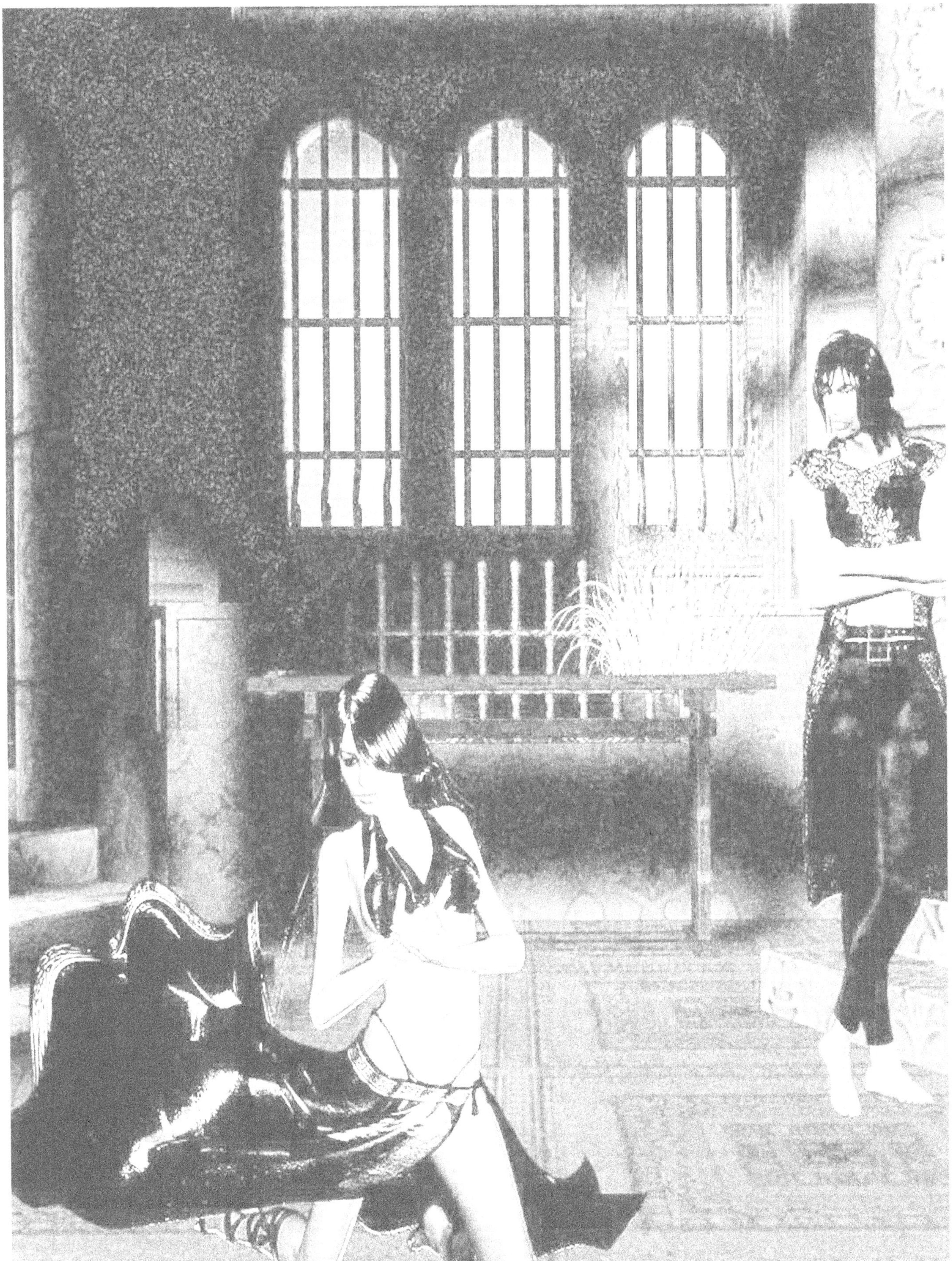

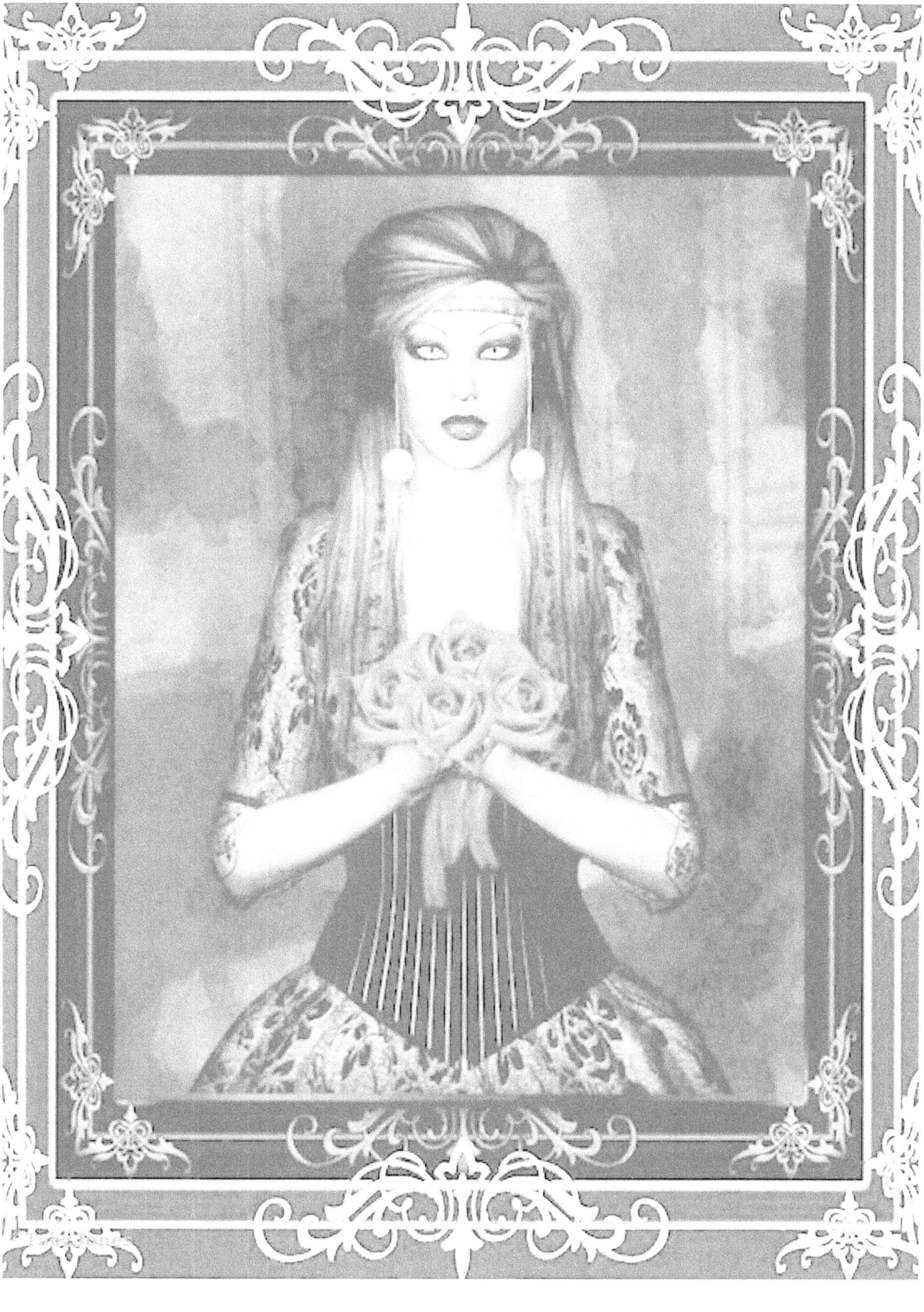

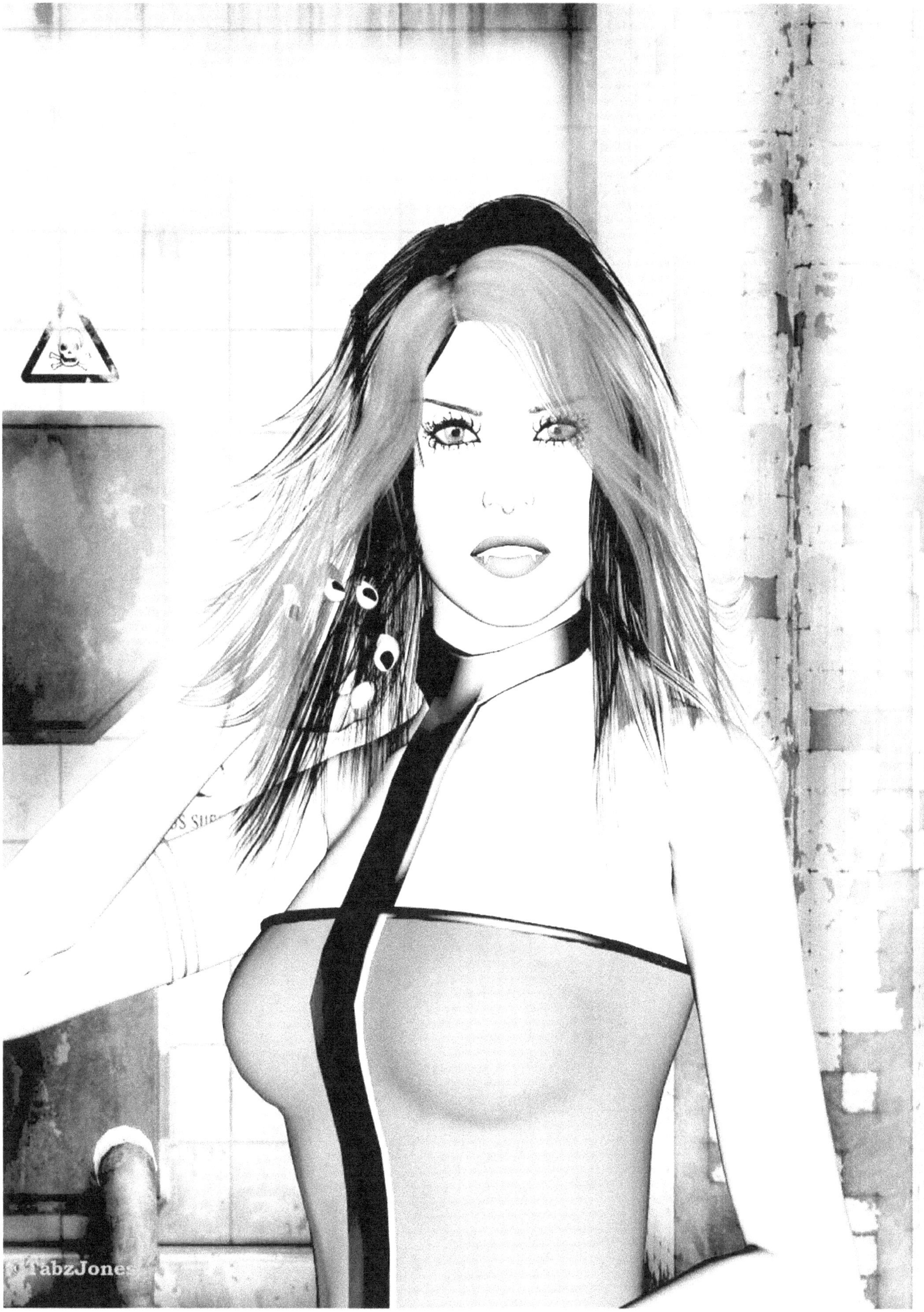
TabzJones

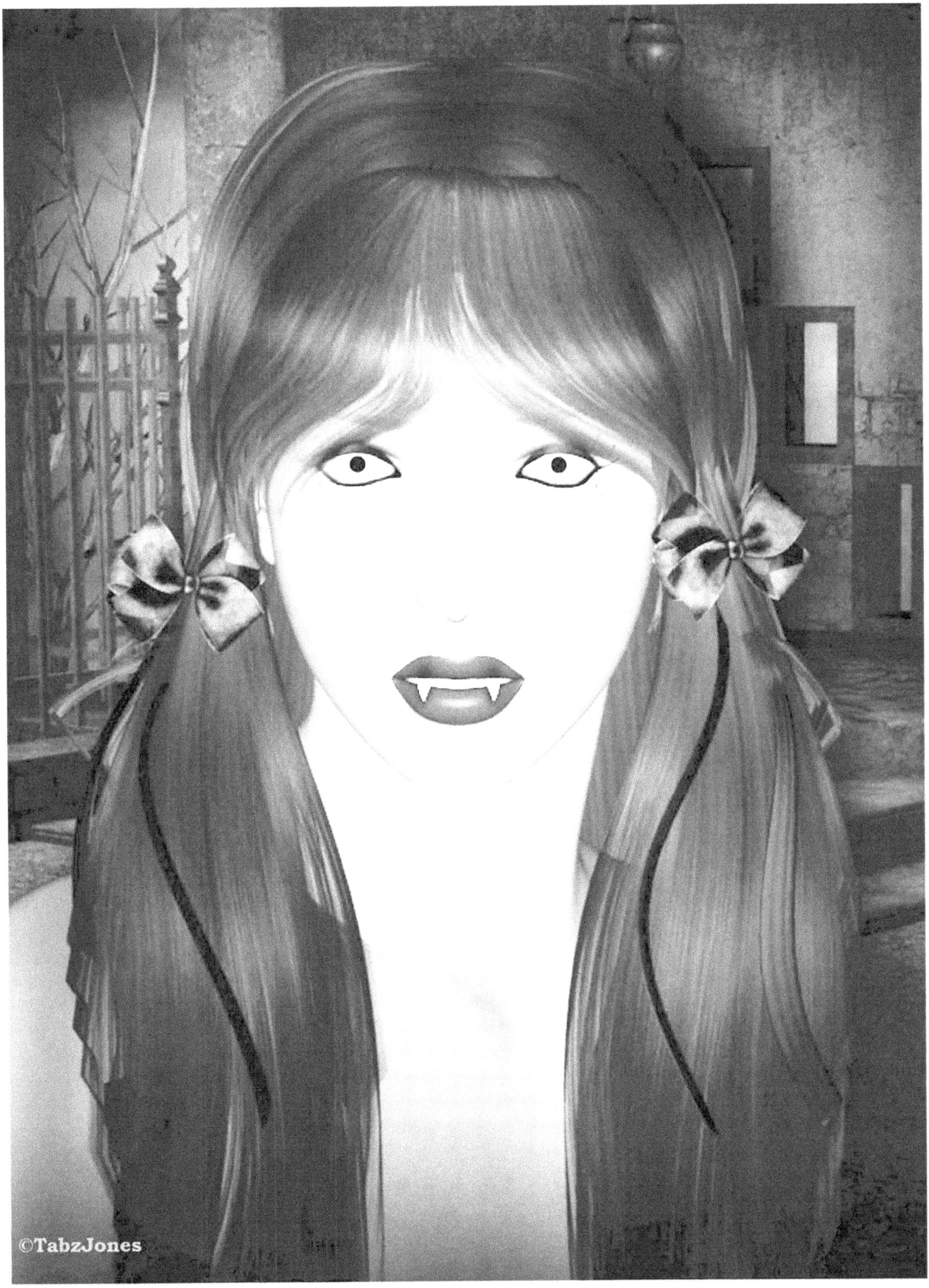
©TabzJones

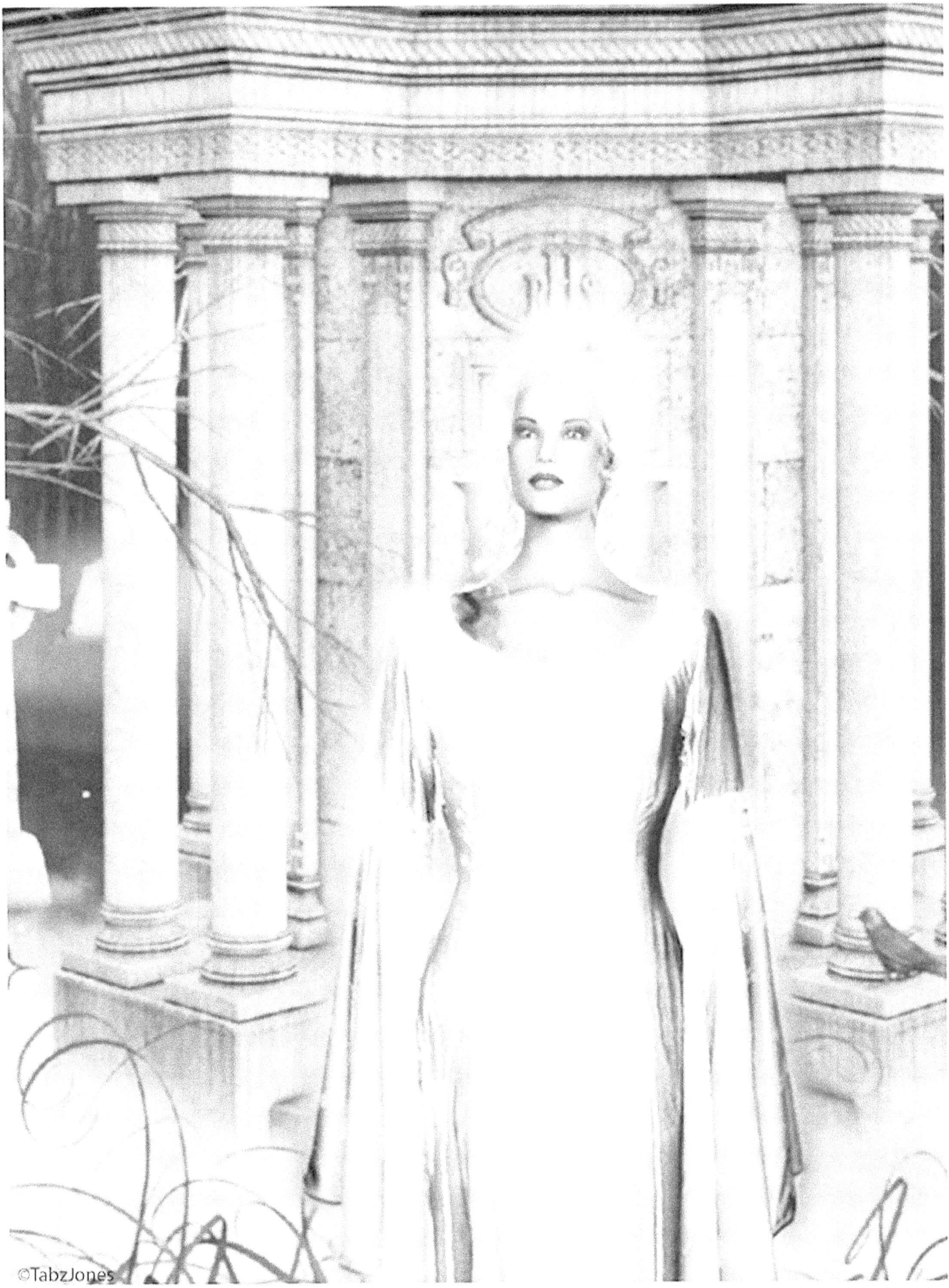
©TabzJones

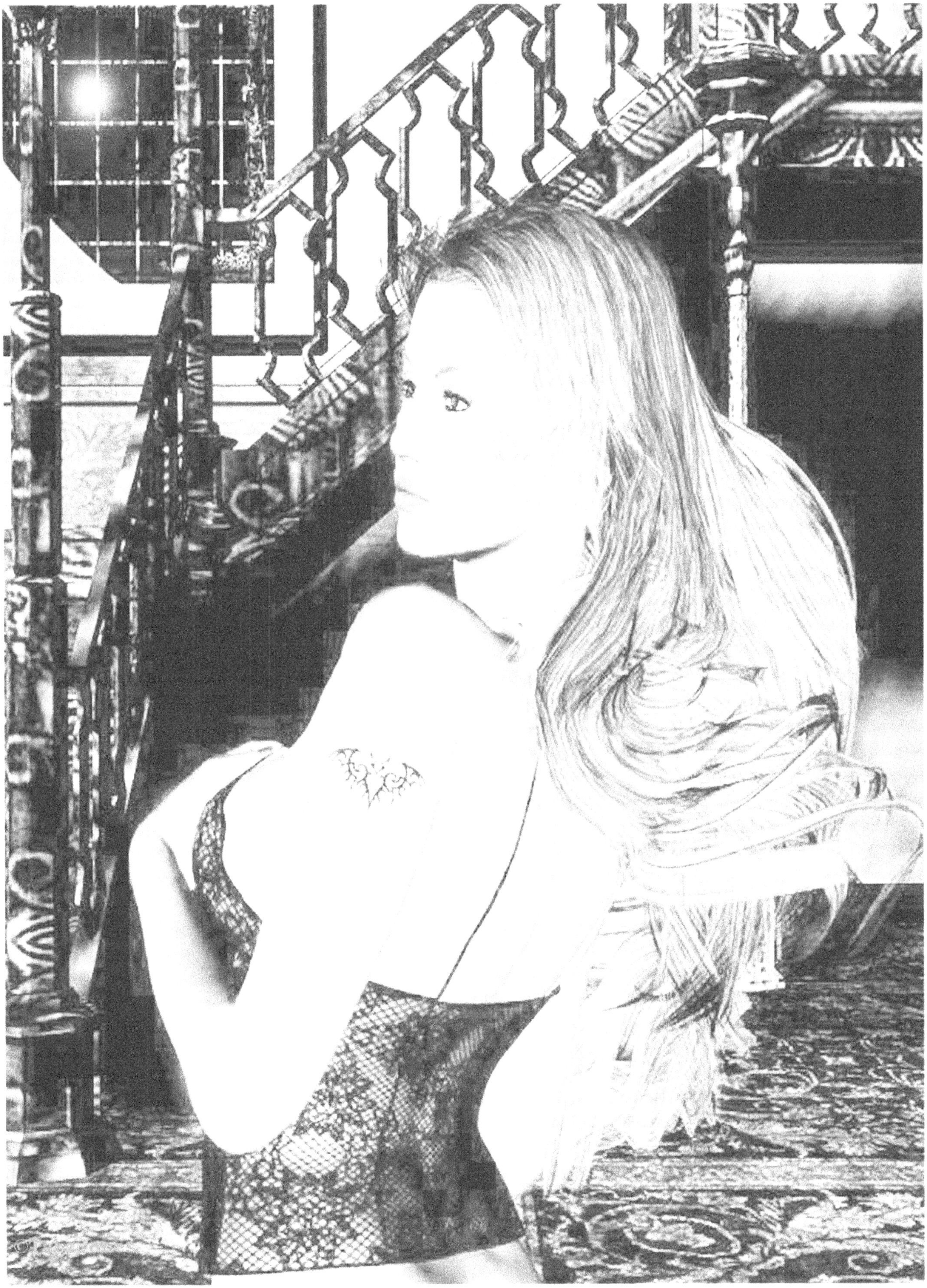

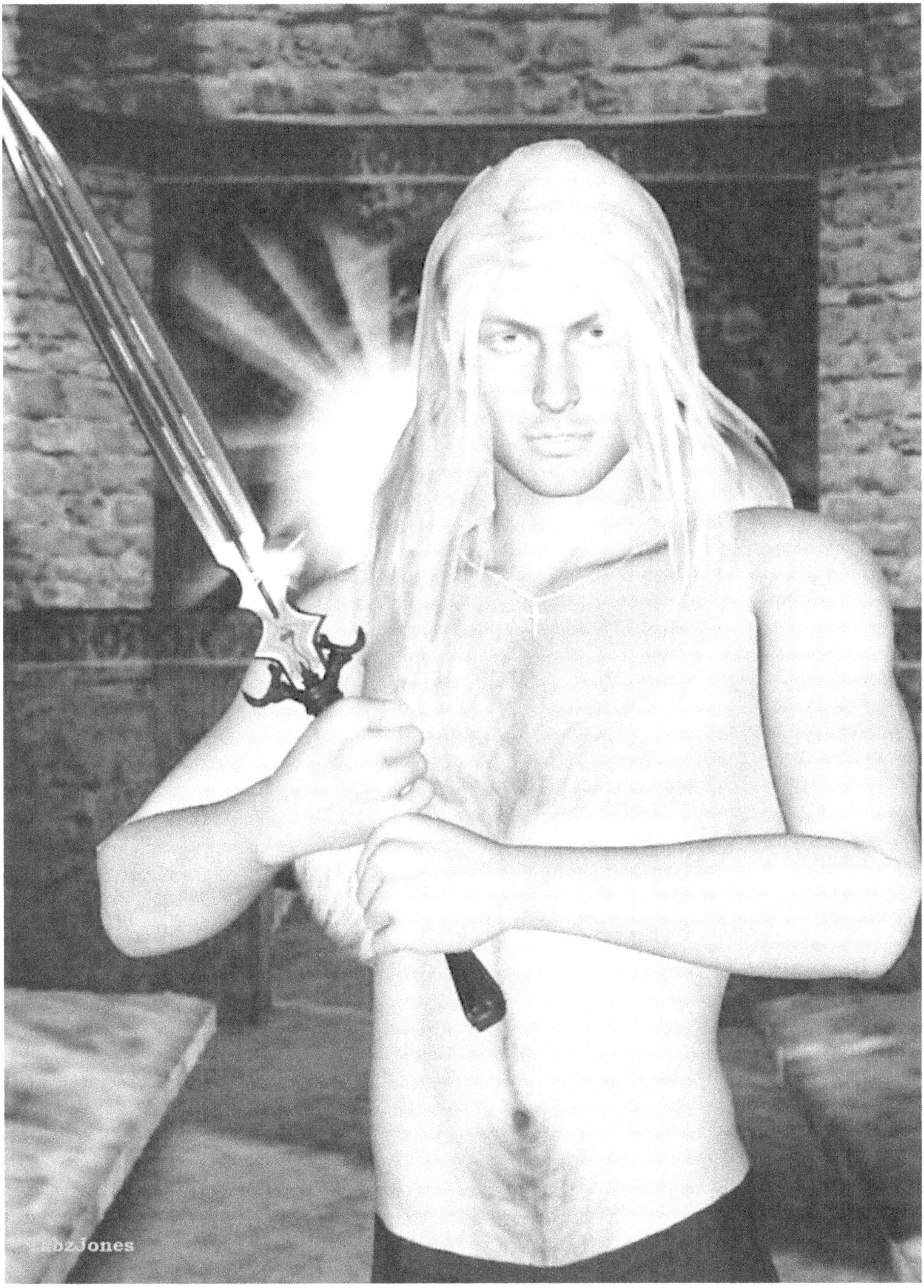

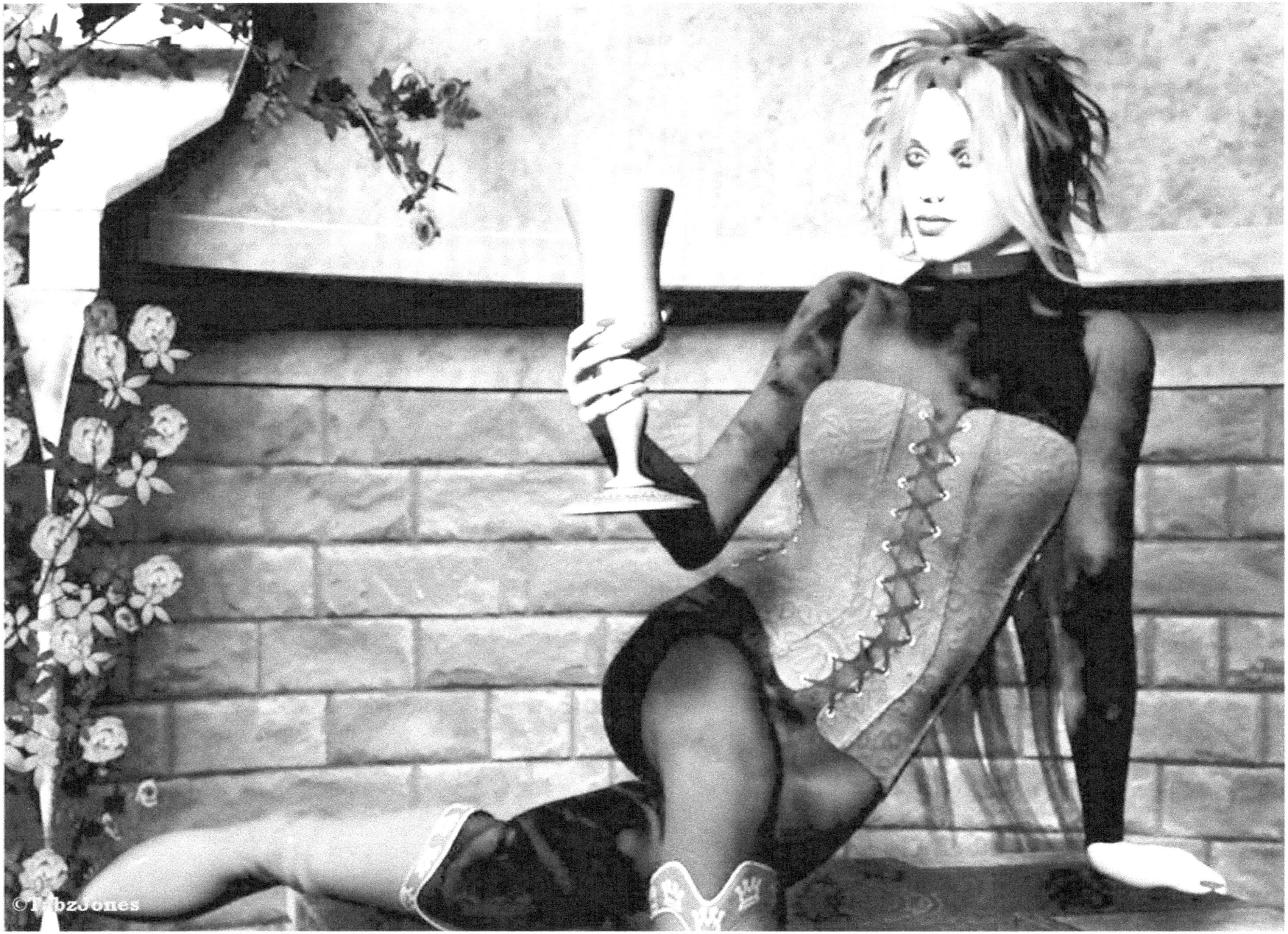

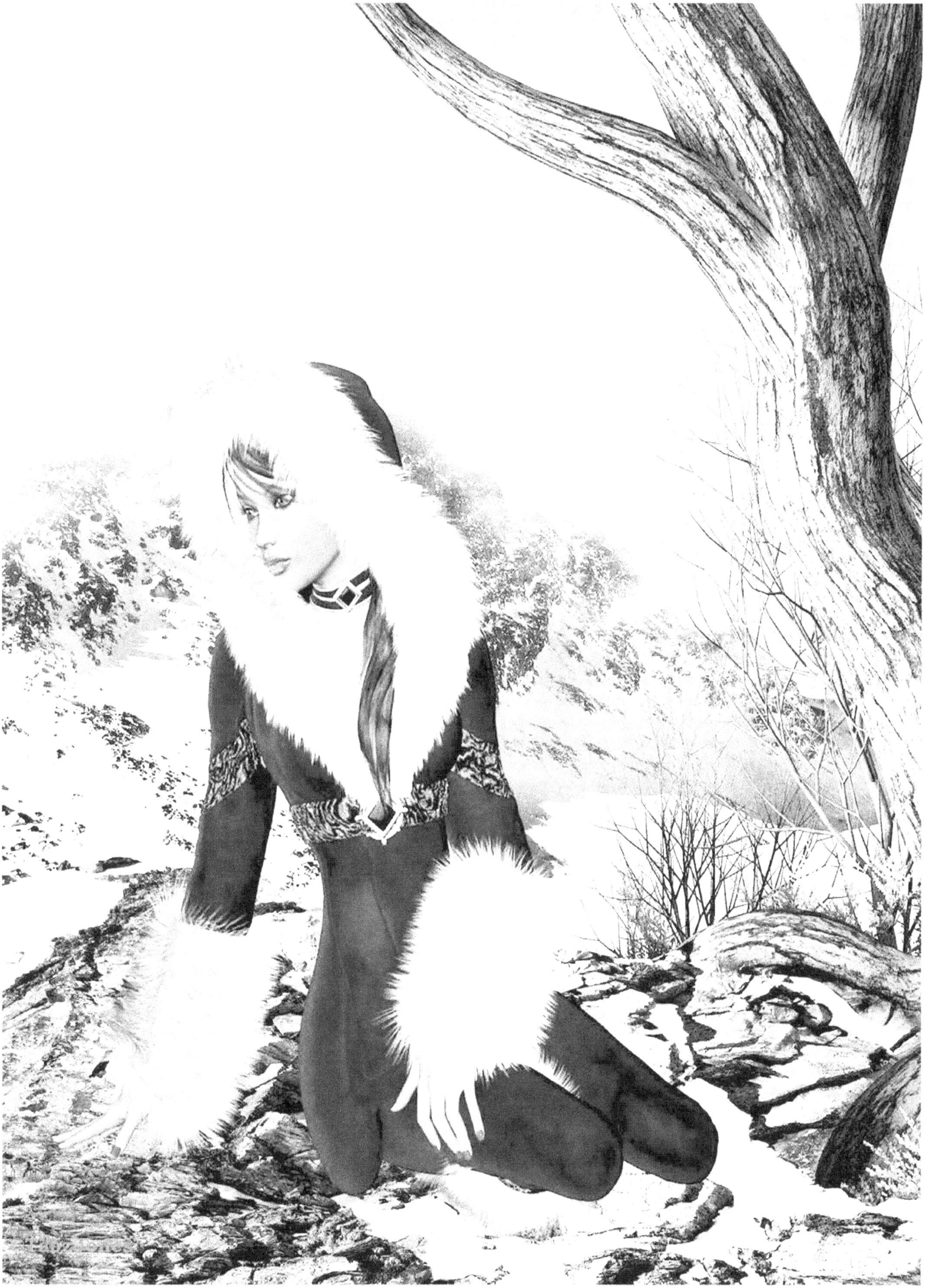

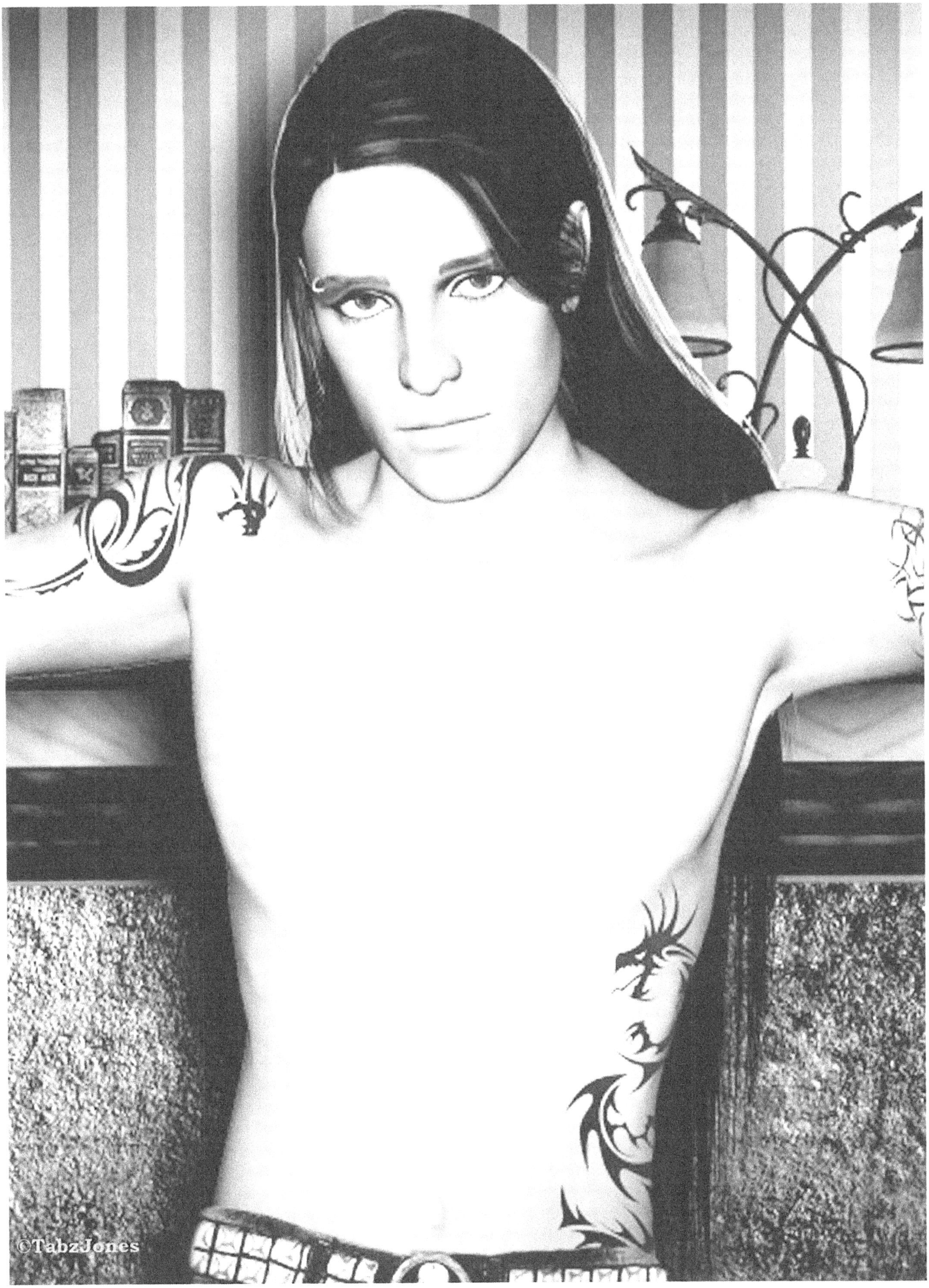
©TabzJones

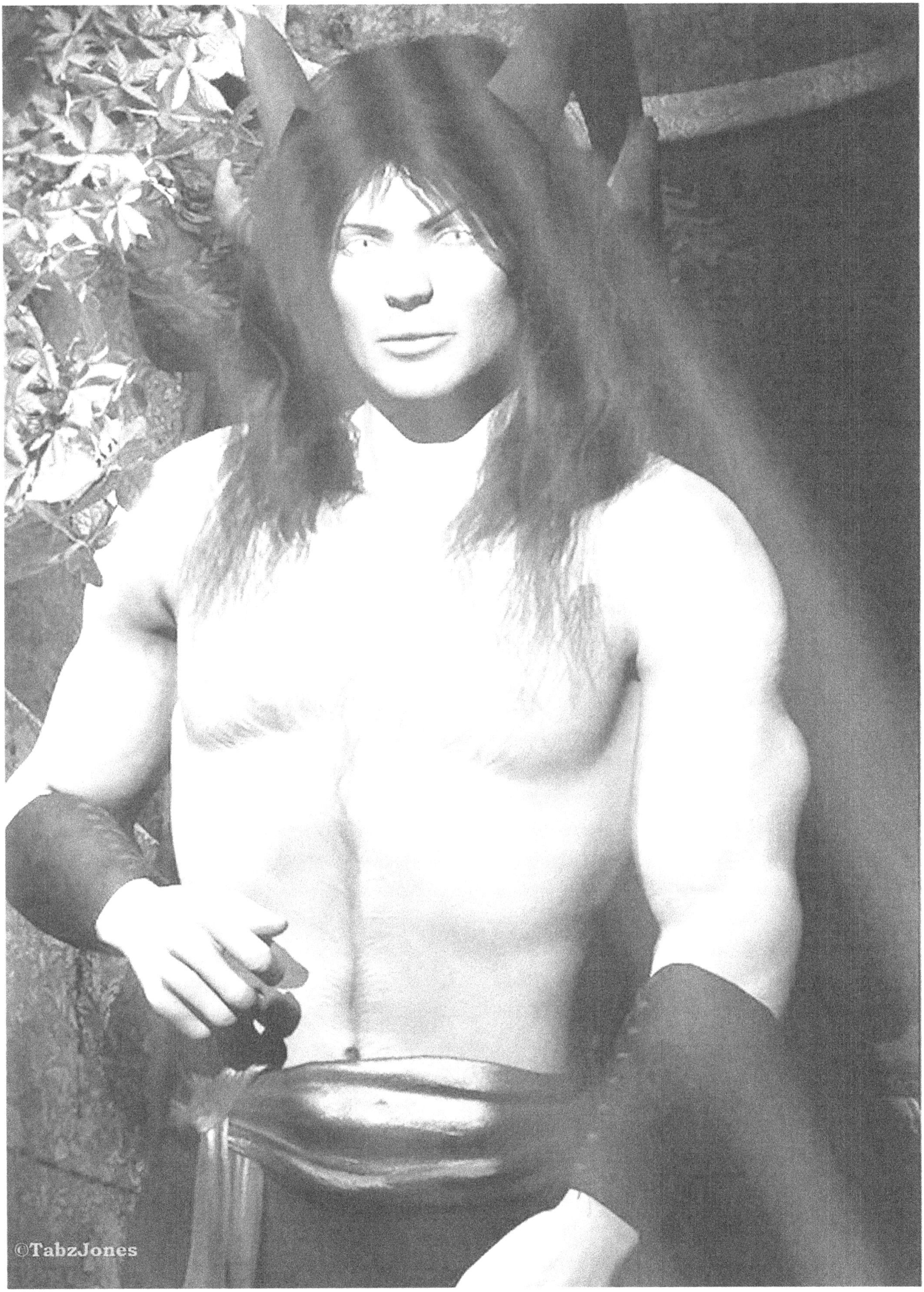
©TabzJones

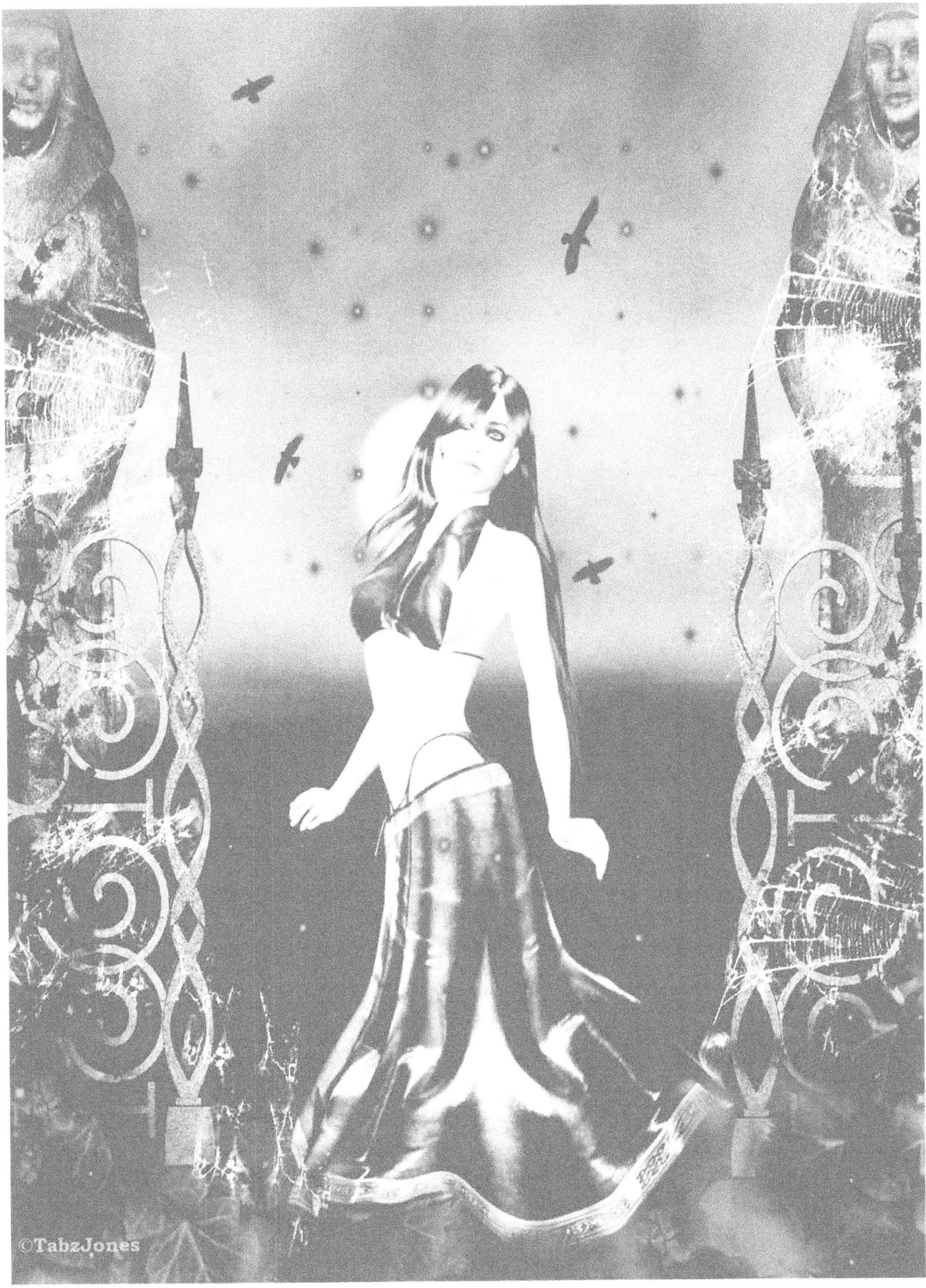
©TabzJones

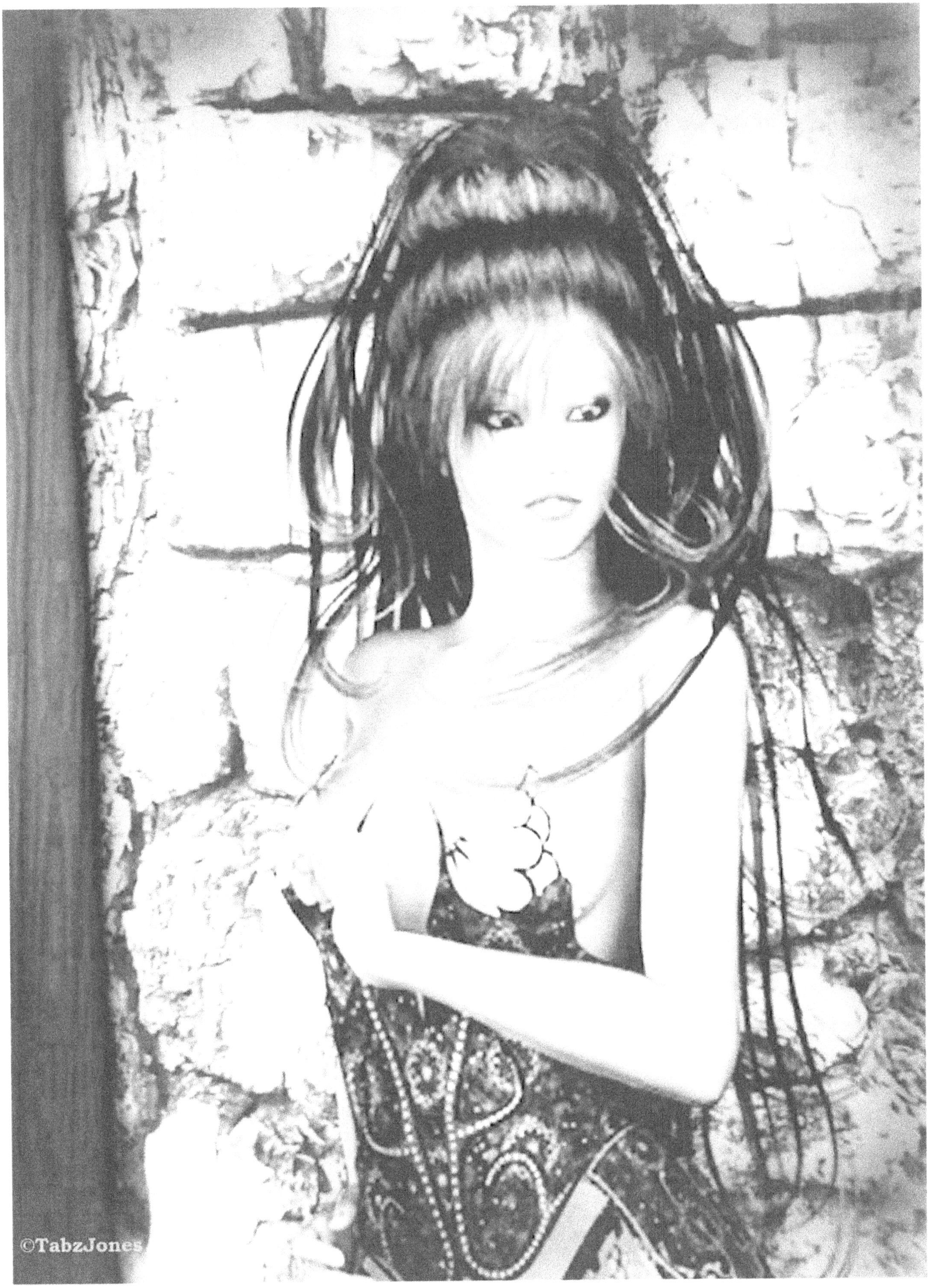
©TabzJones

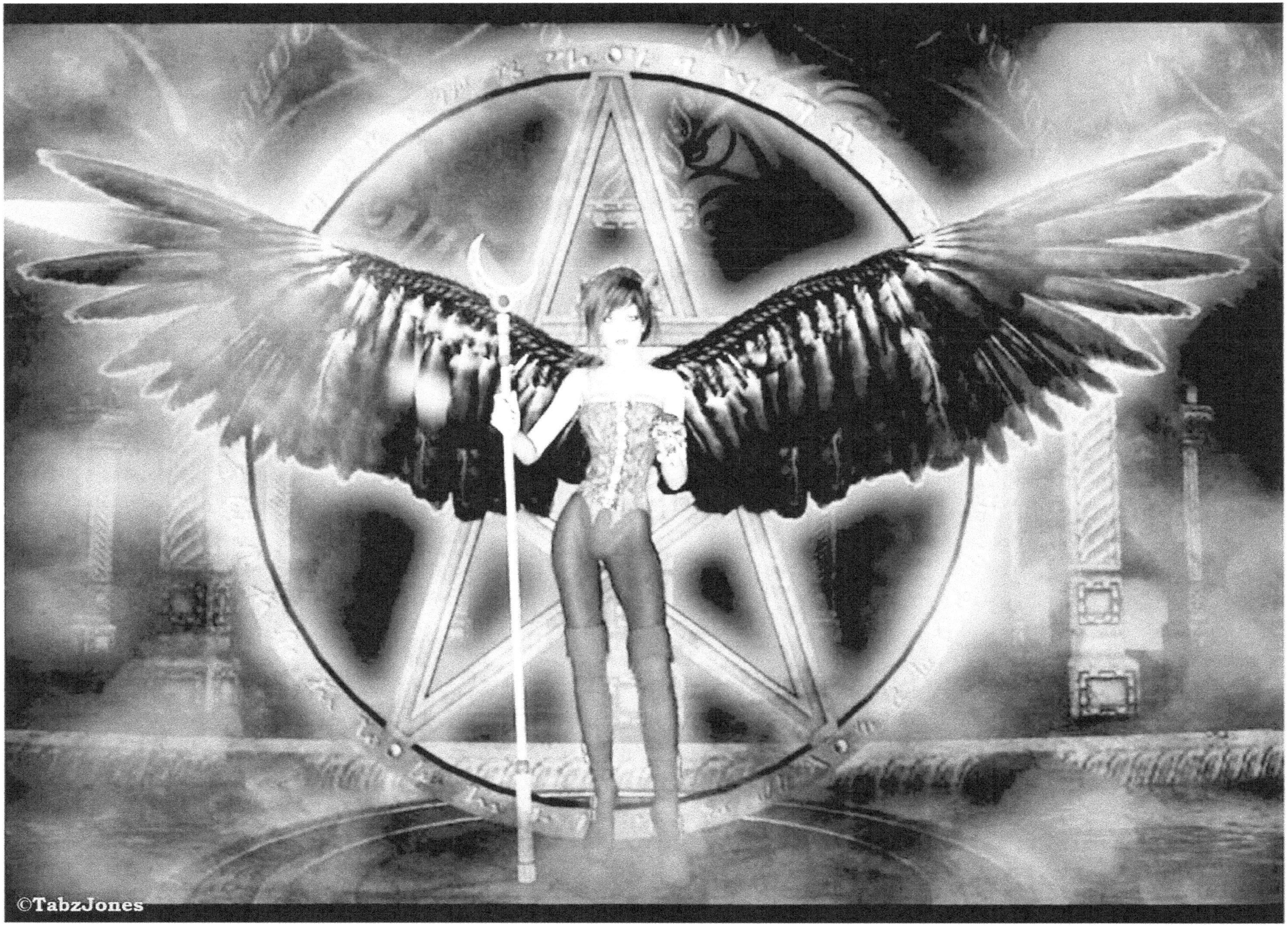
©TabzJones

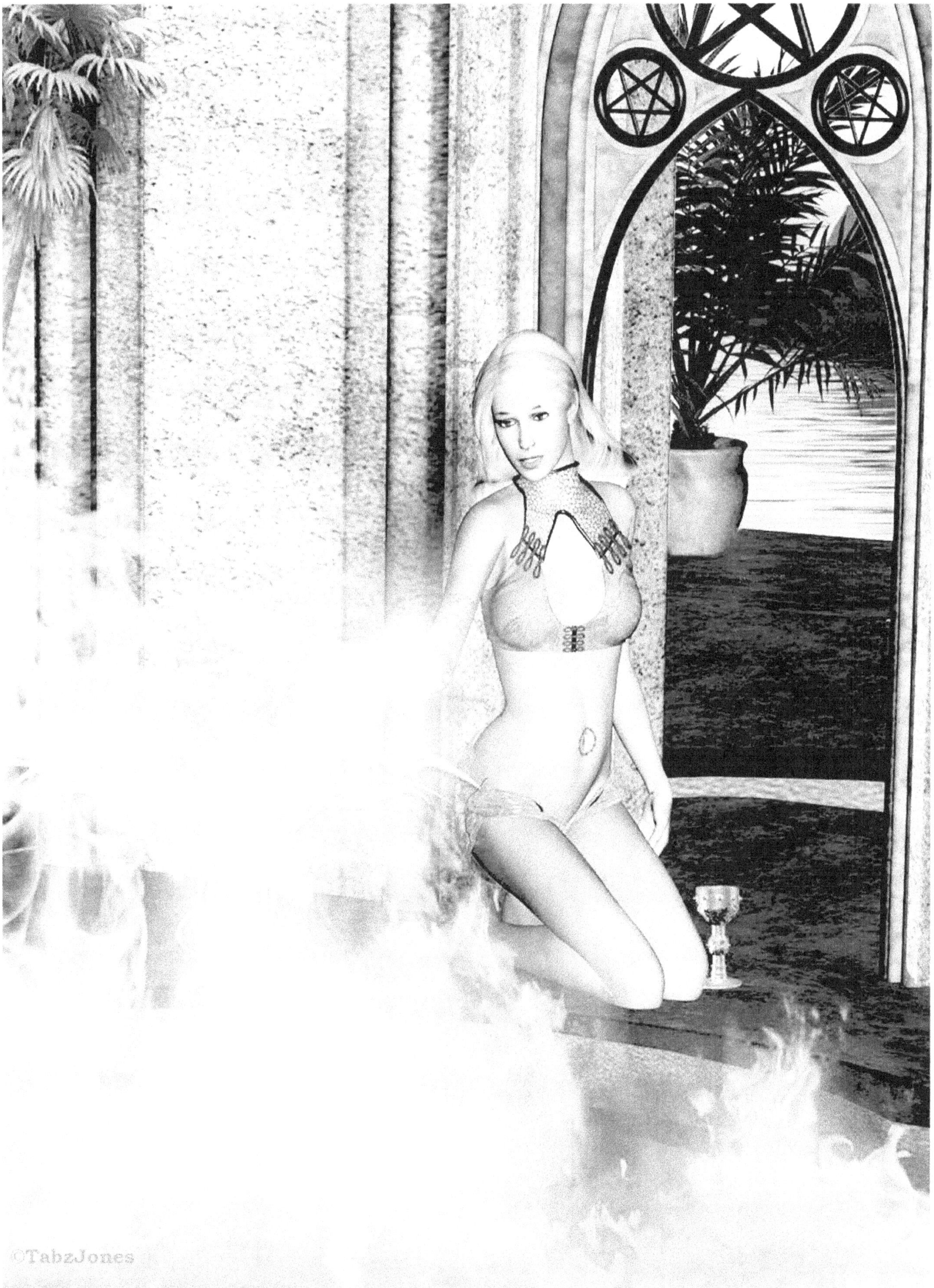
©TabzJones

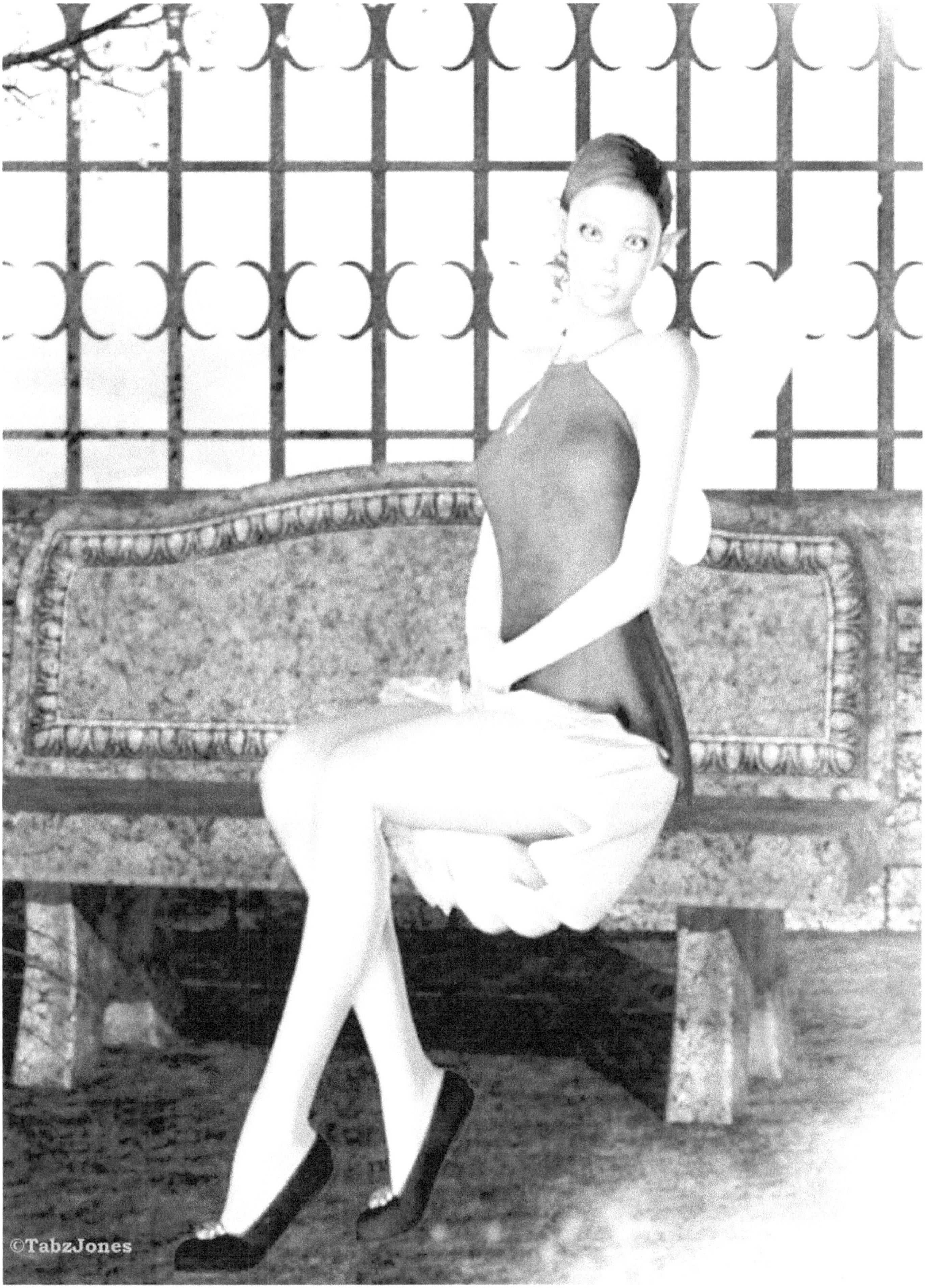
©TabzJones

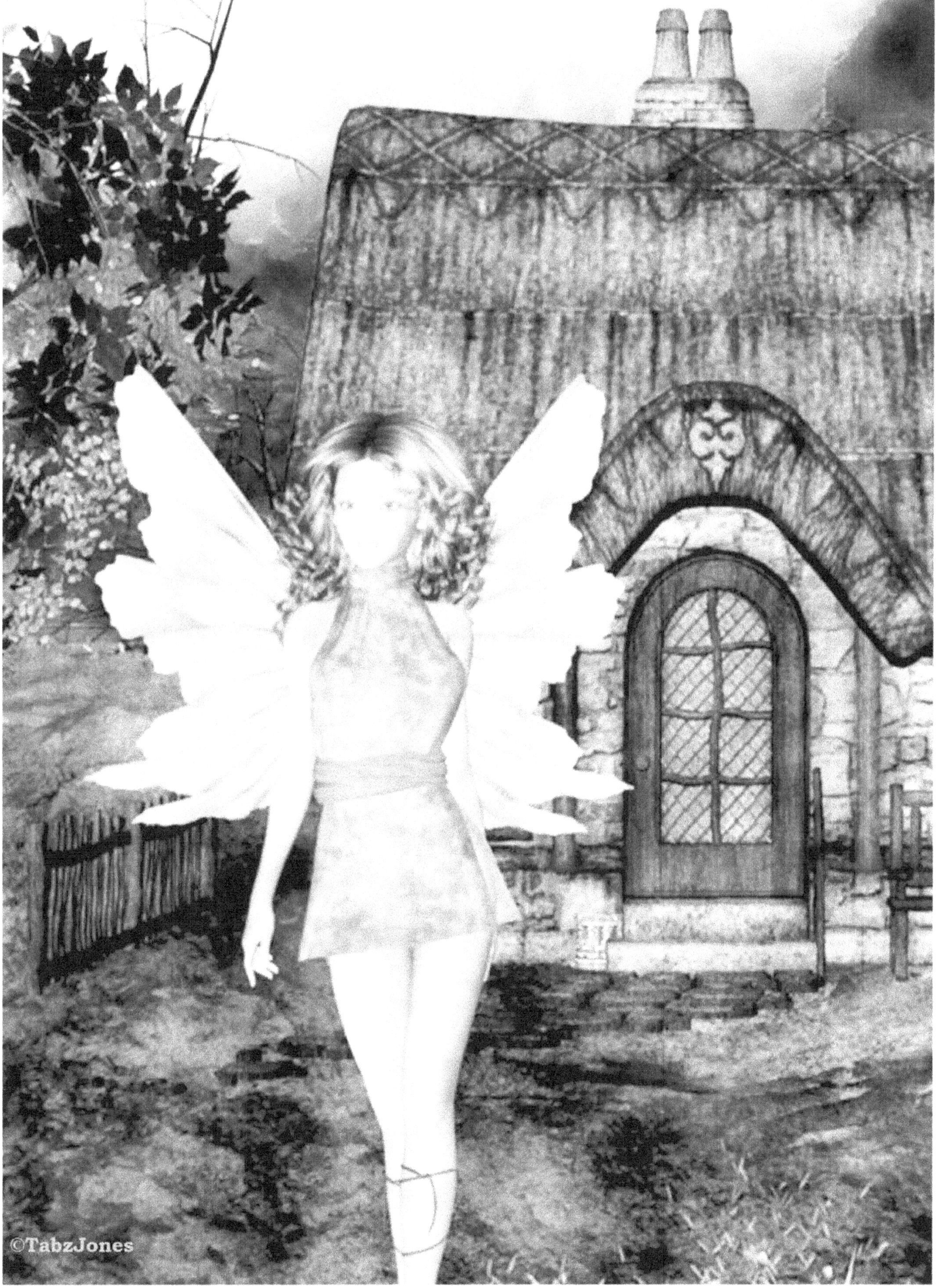
©TabzJones

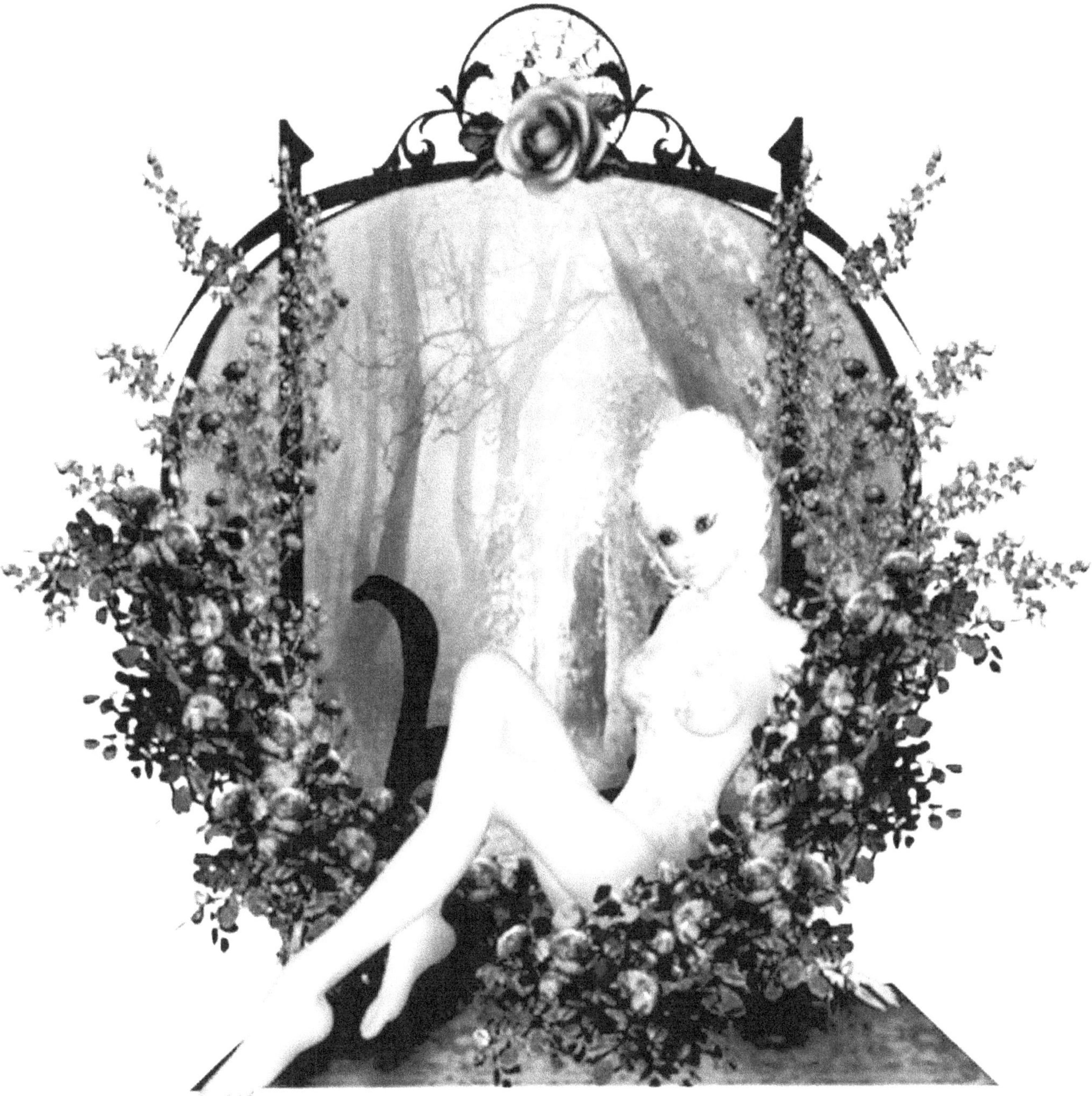

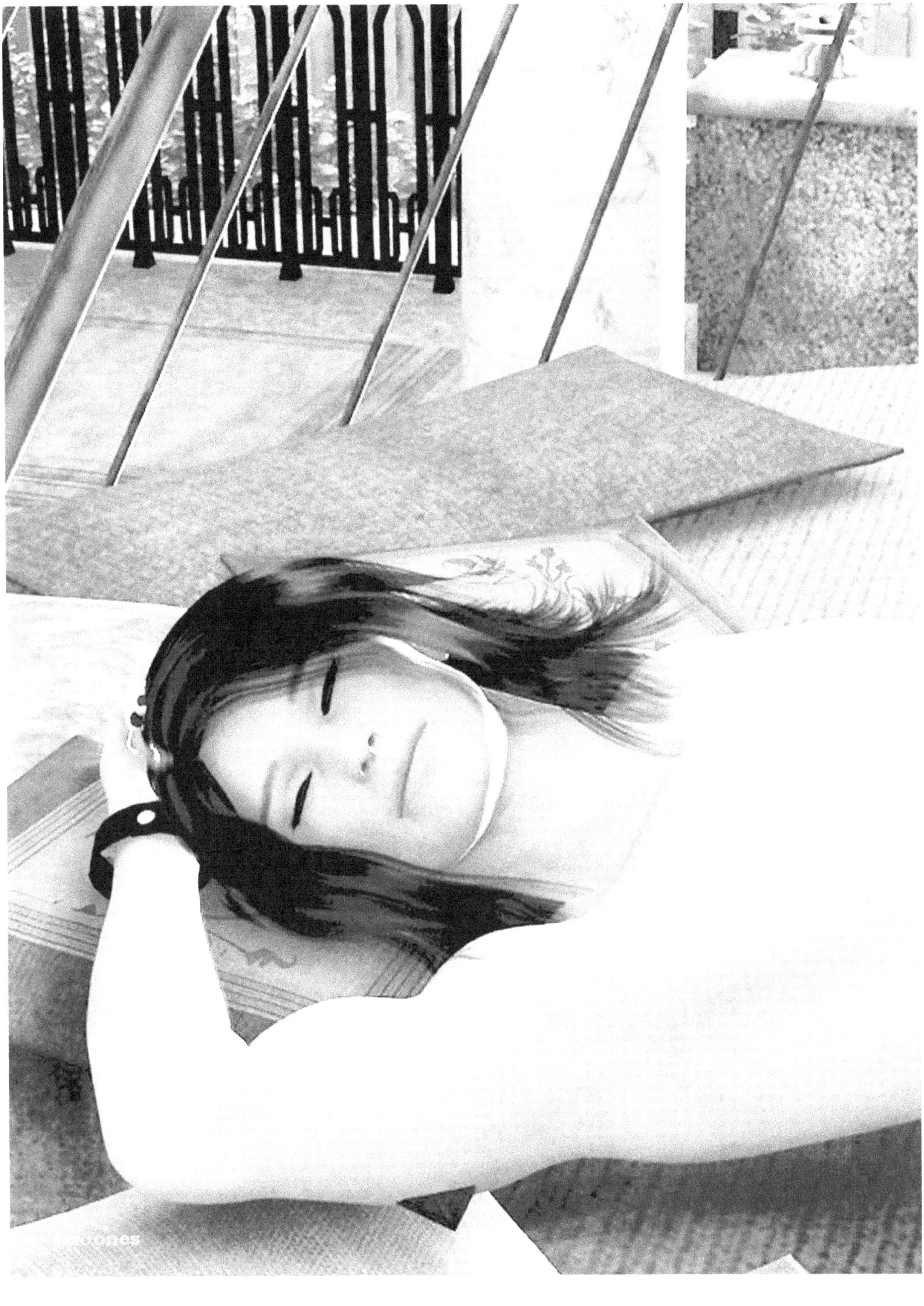

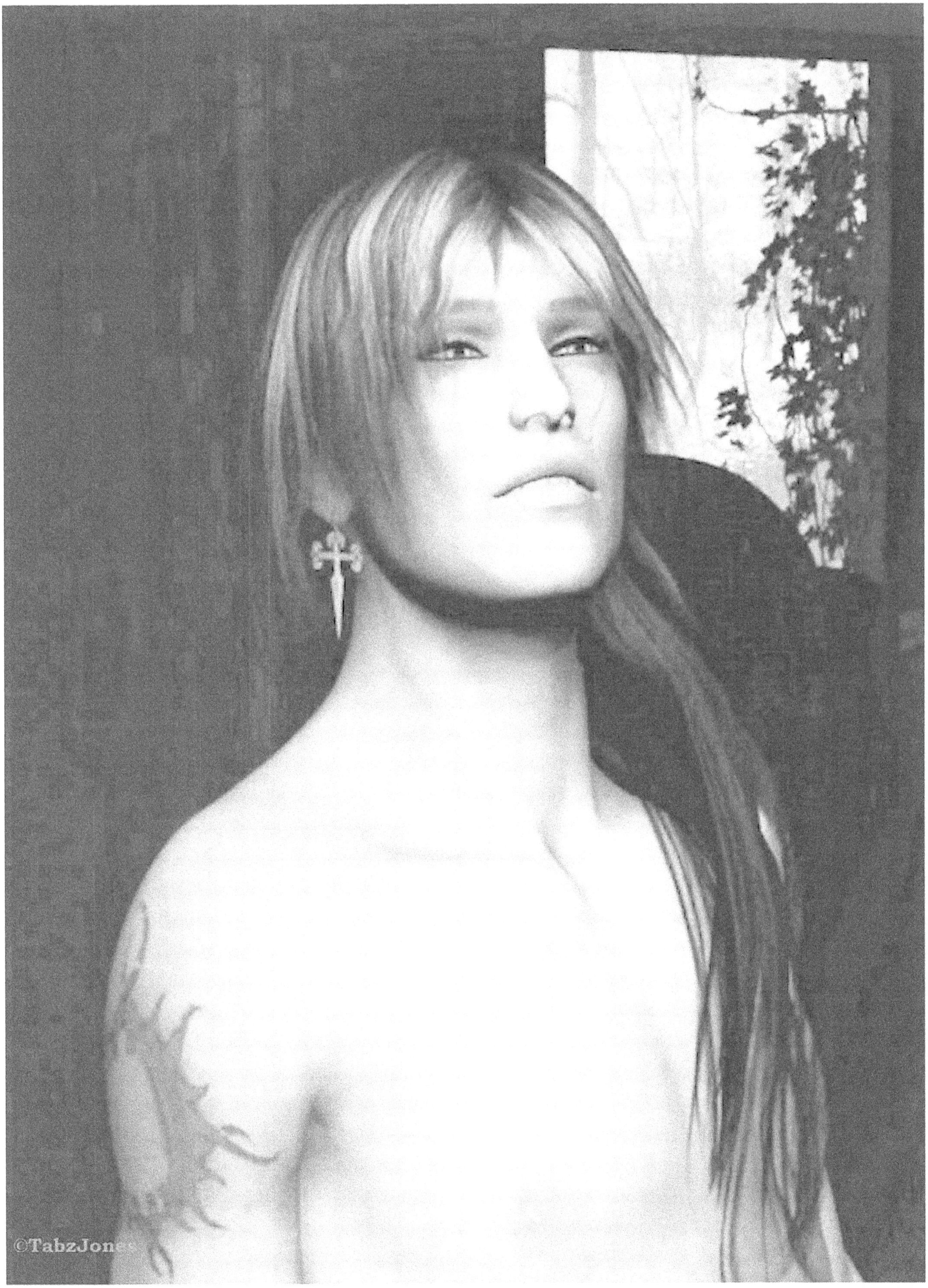
©TabzJones

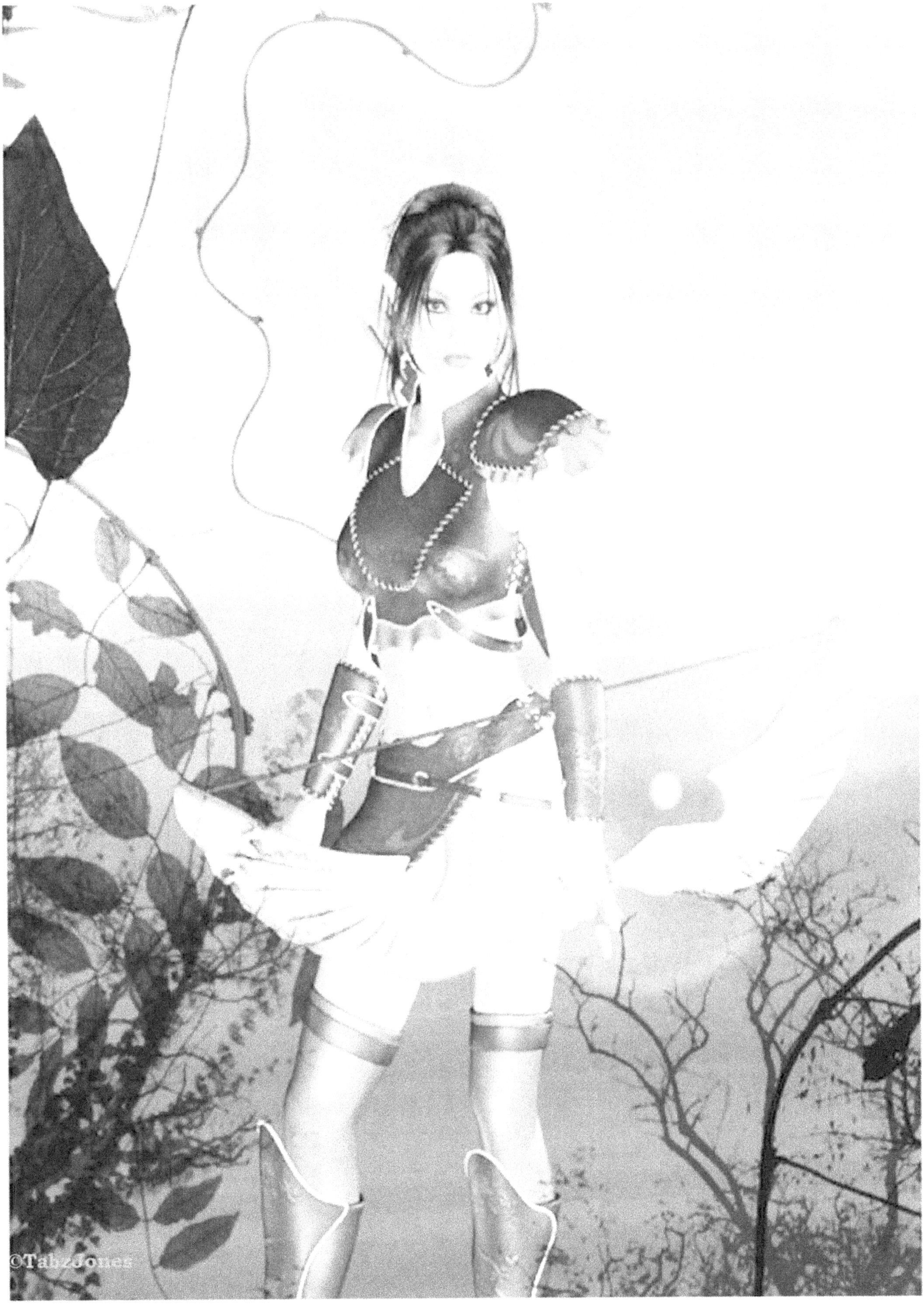
©TabzJones

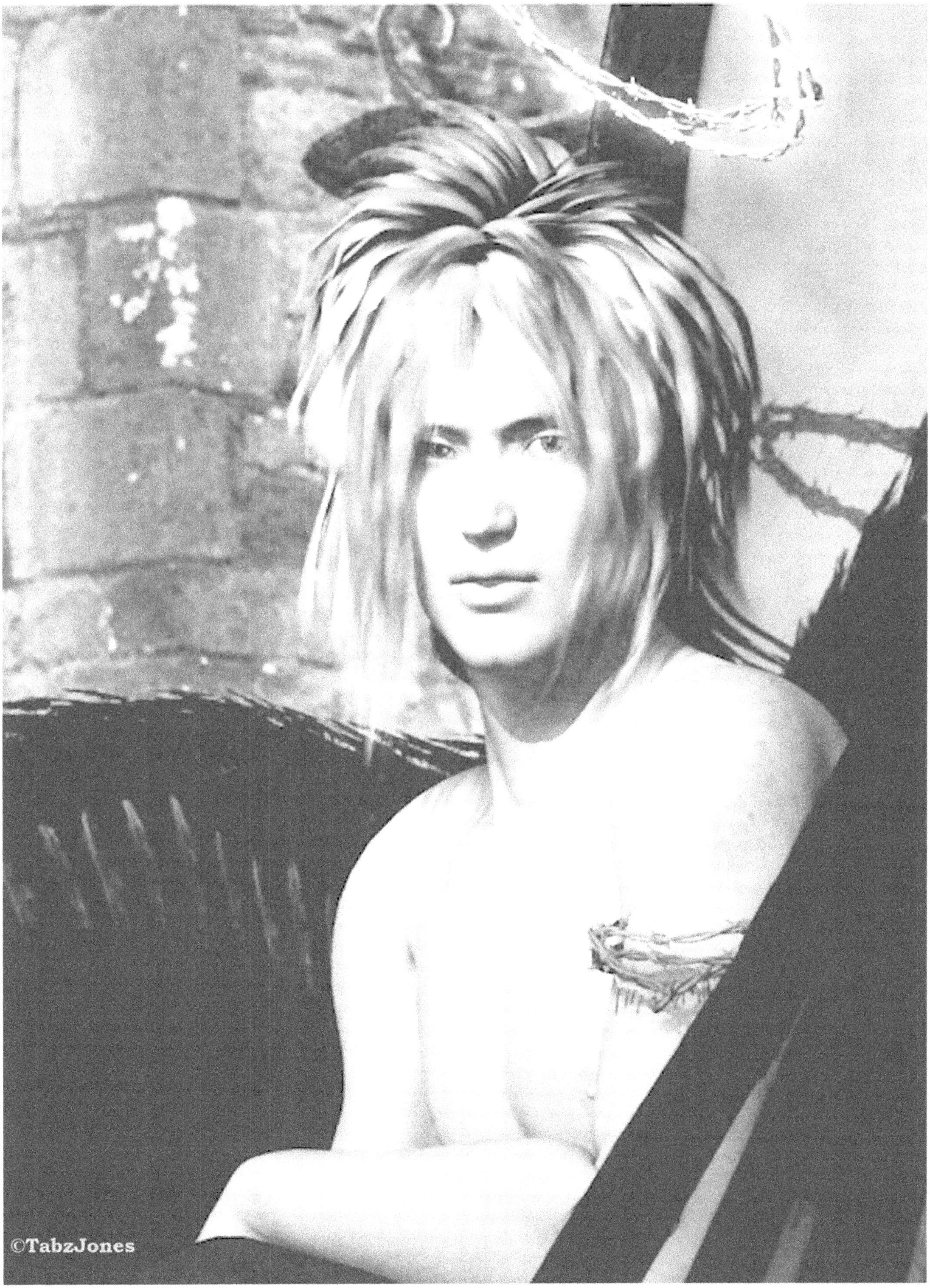
©TabzJones

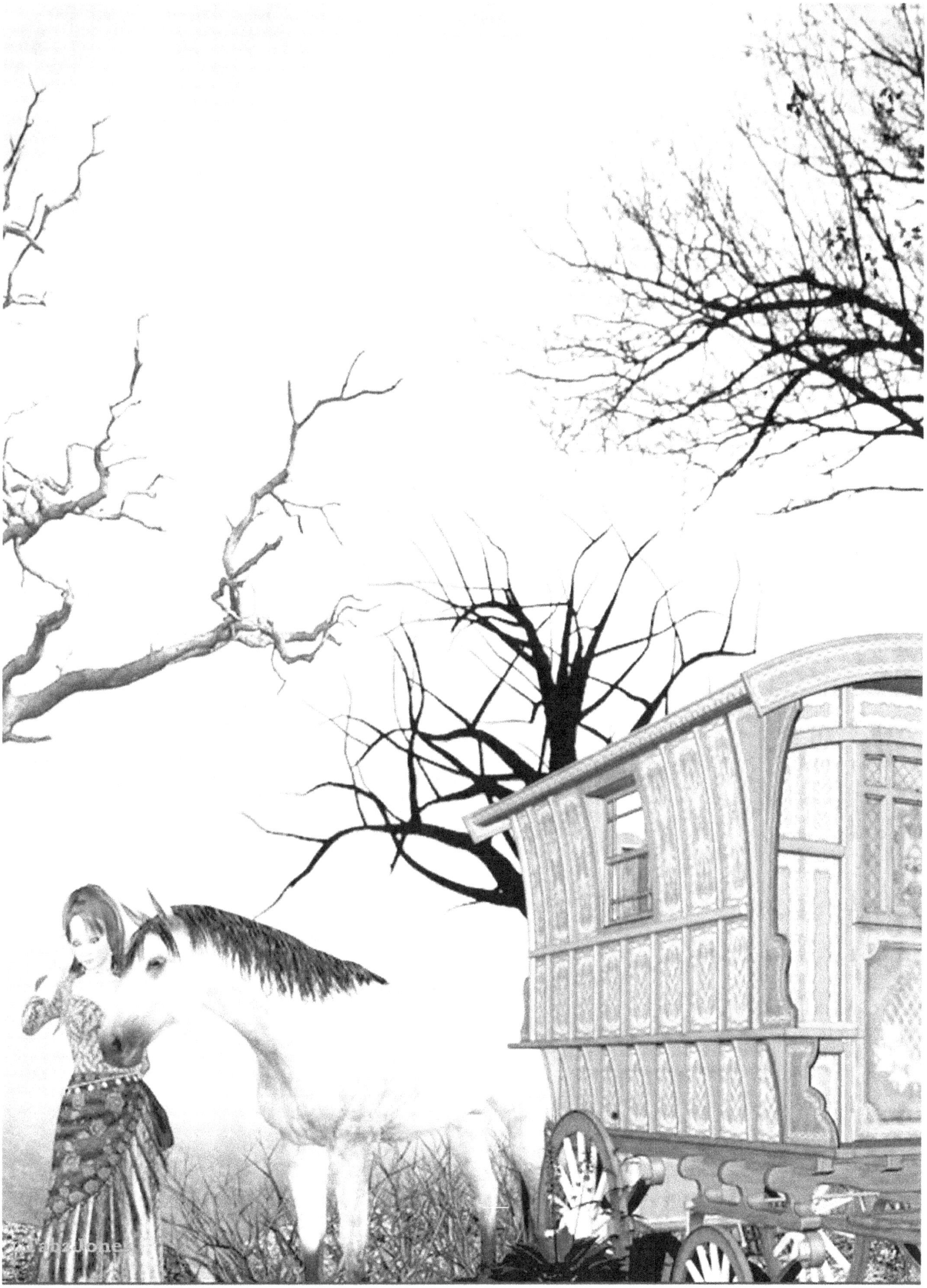

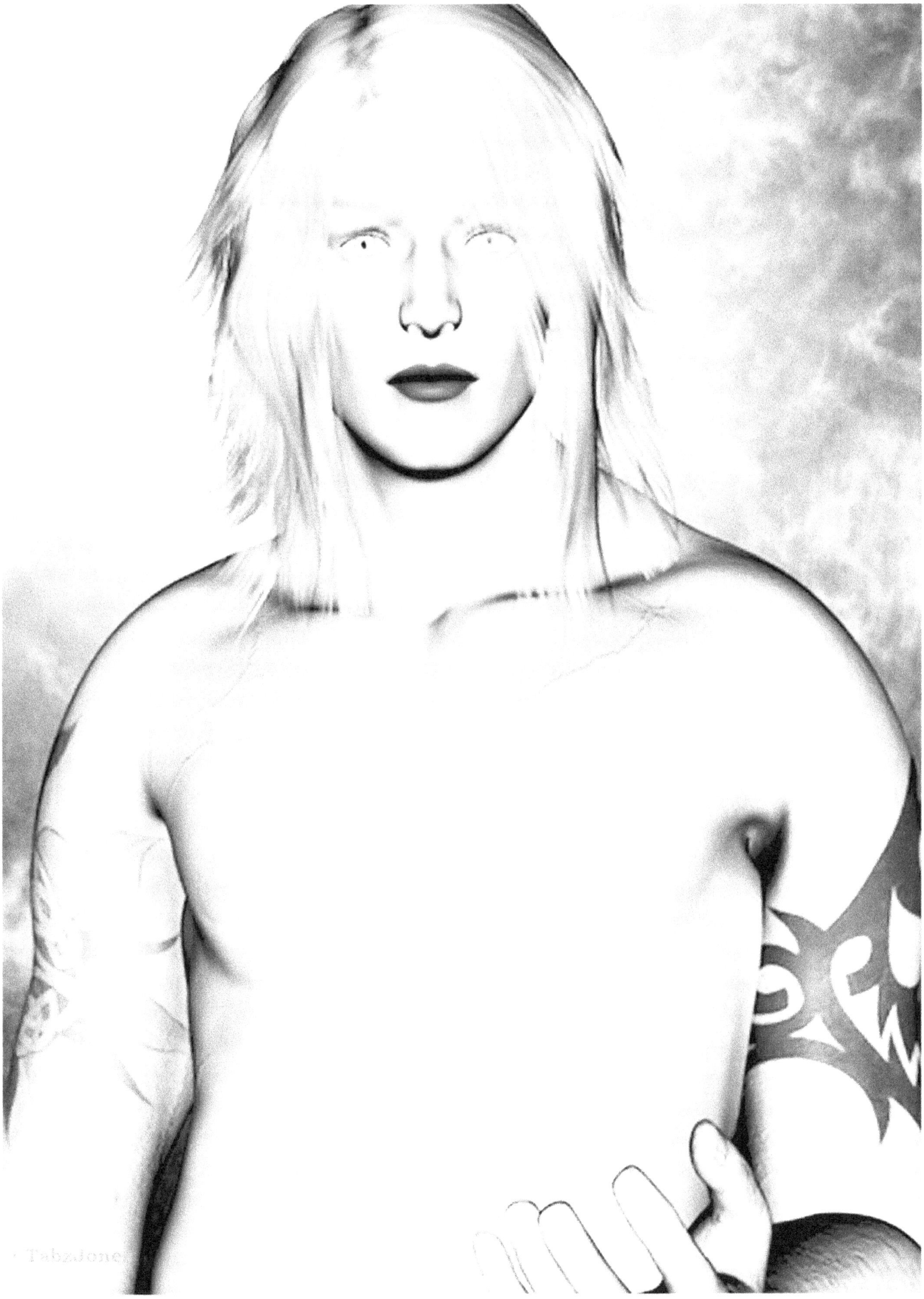

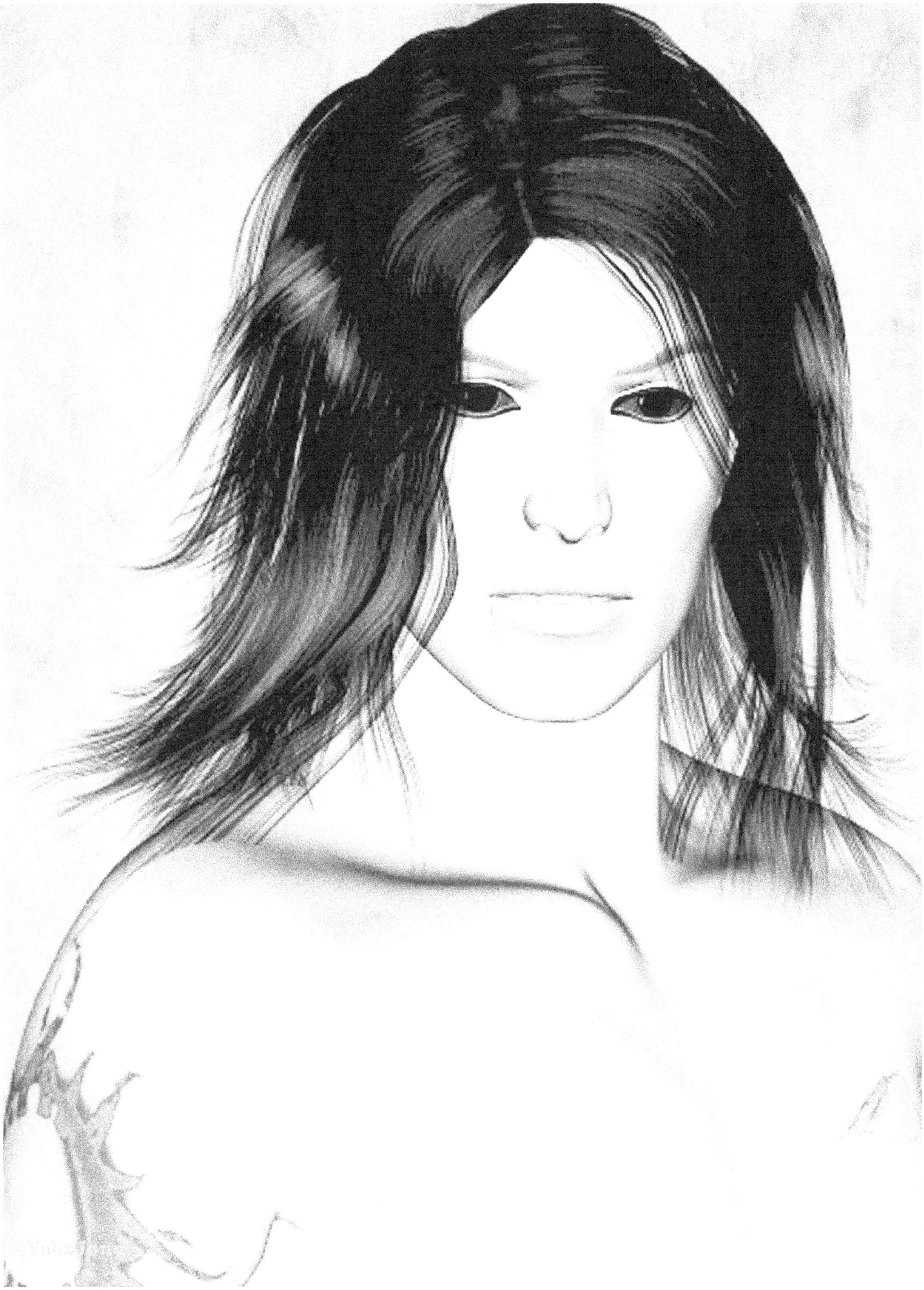

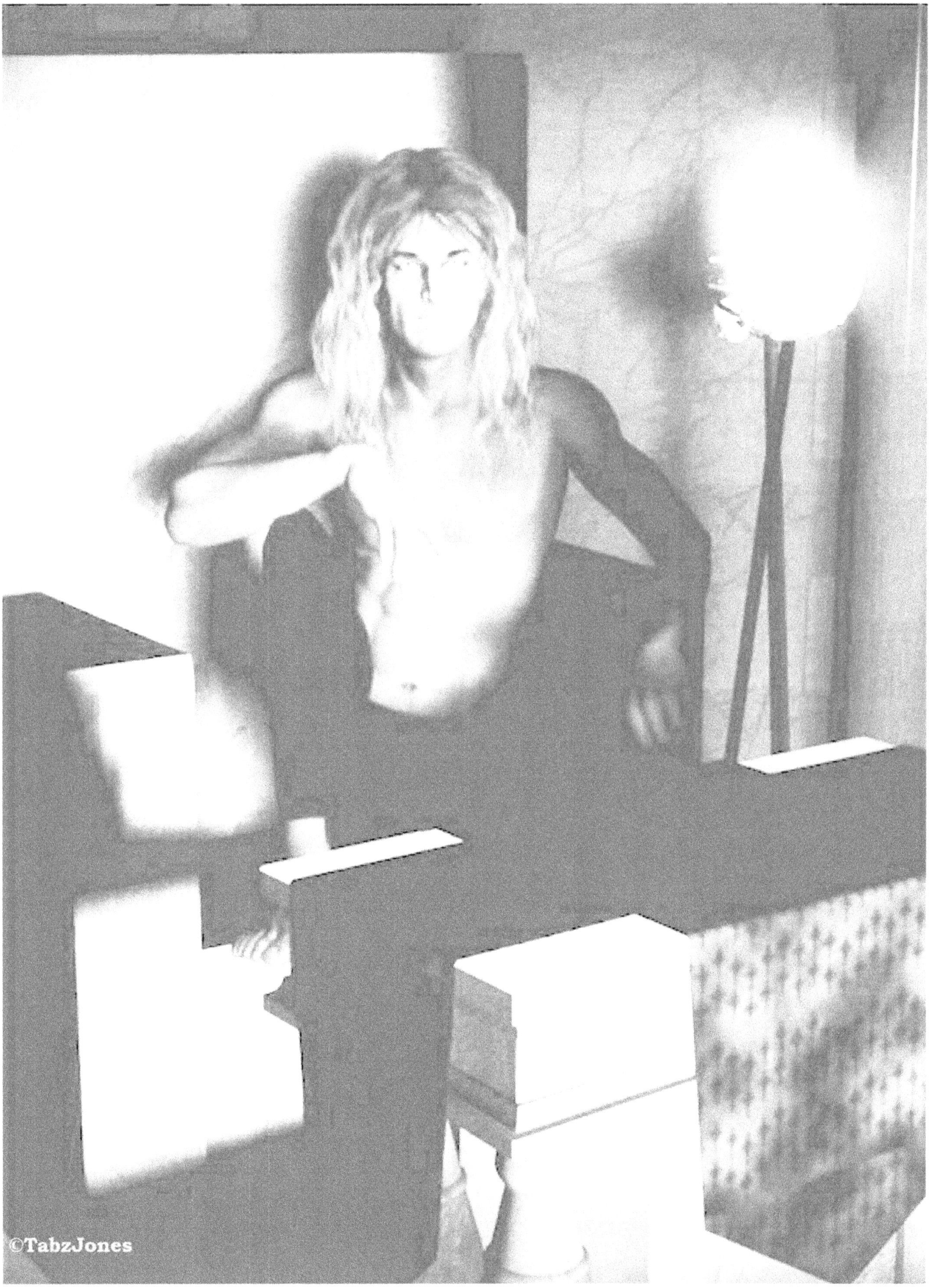
©TabzJones

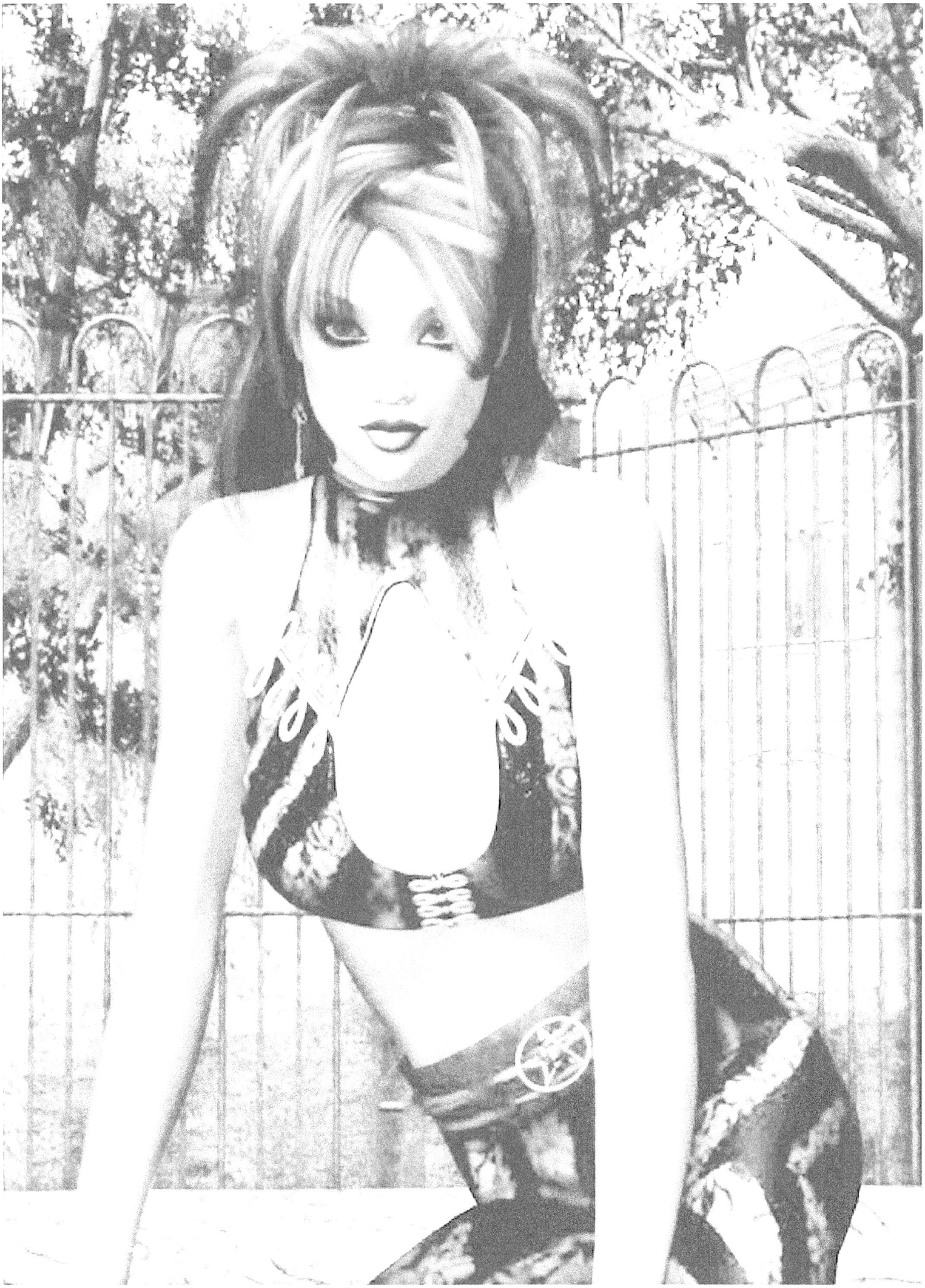

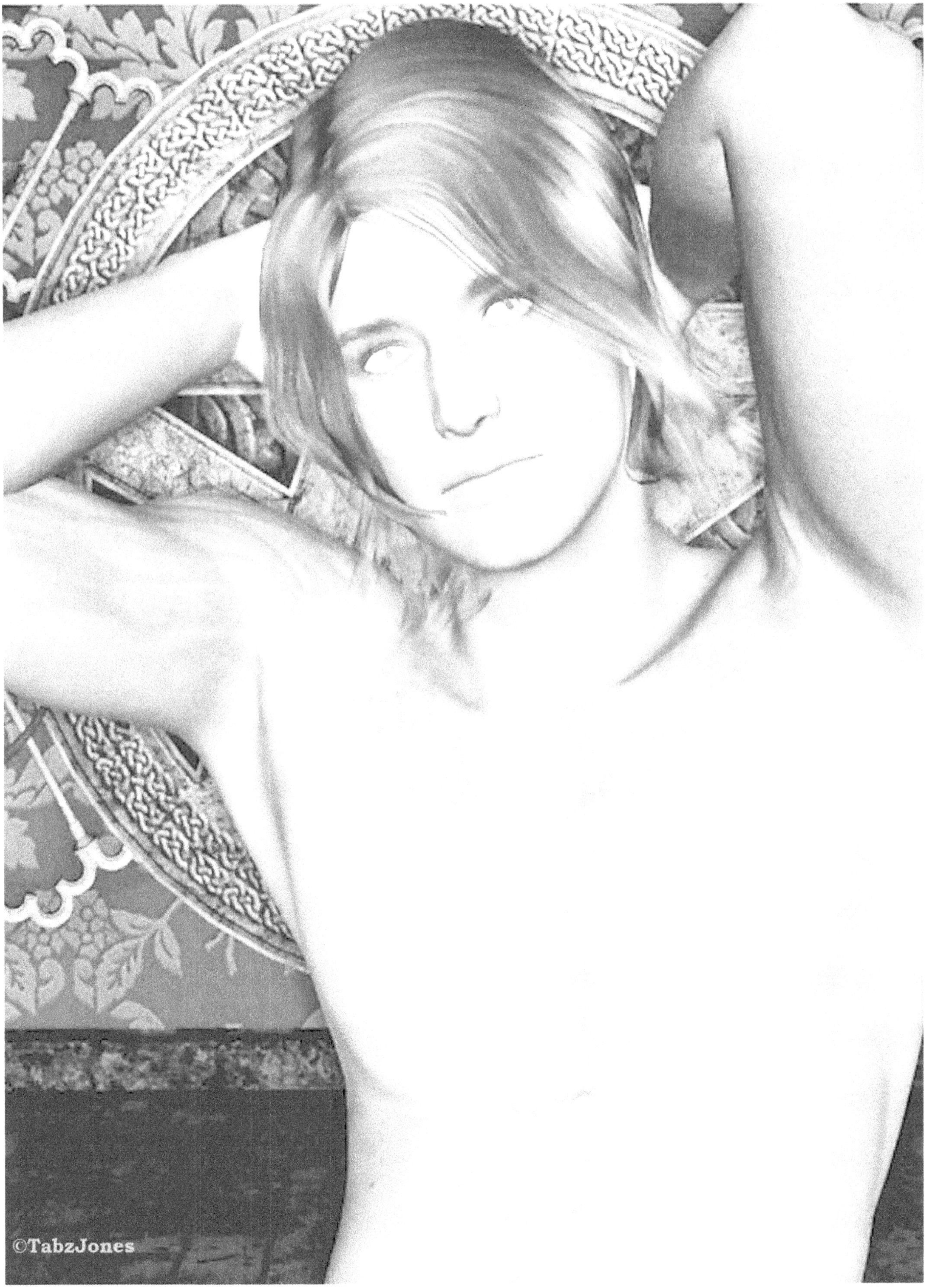
©TabzJones

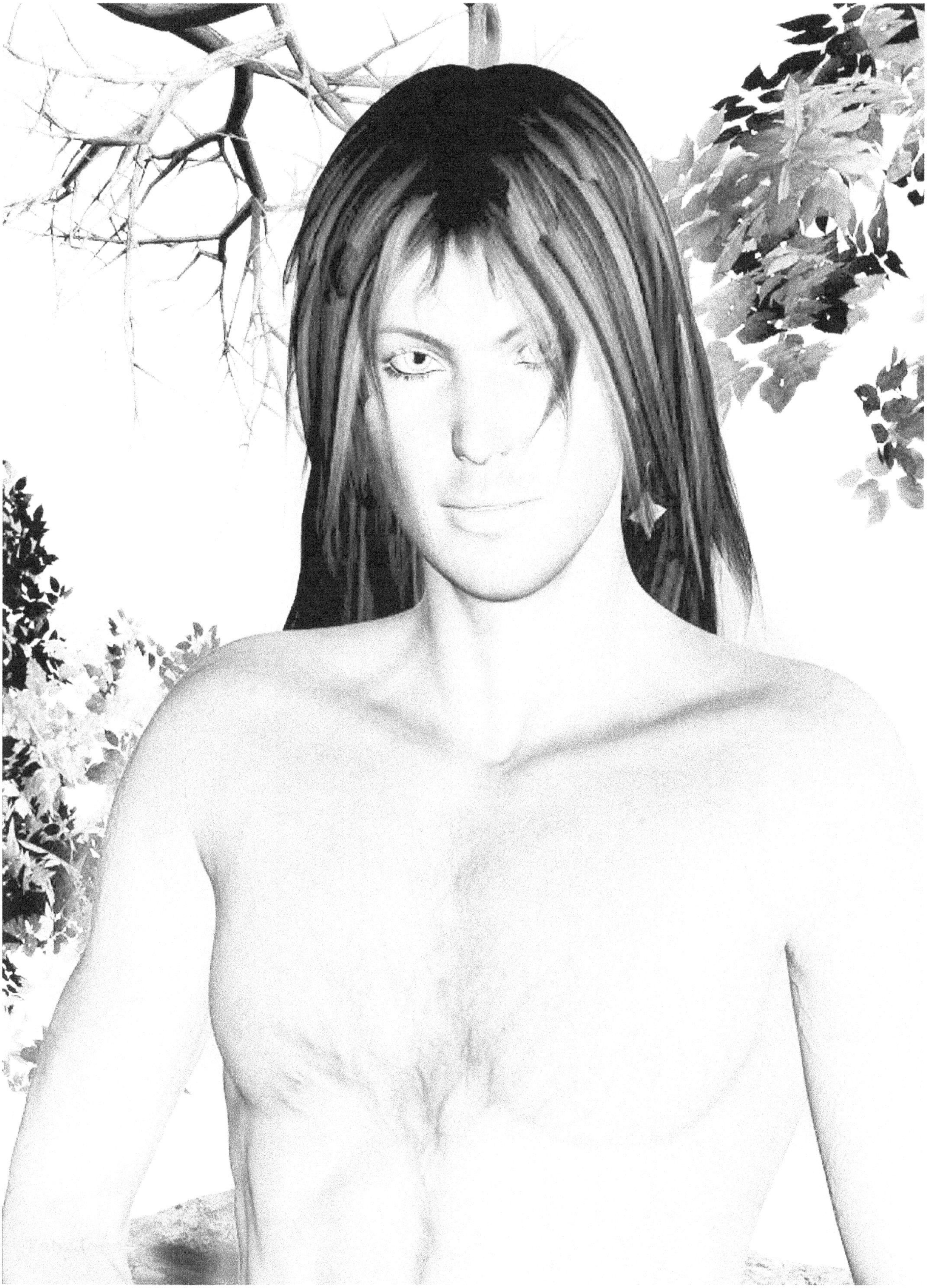

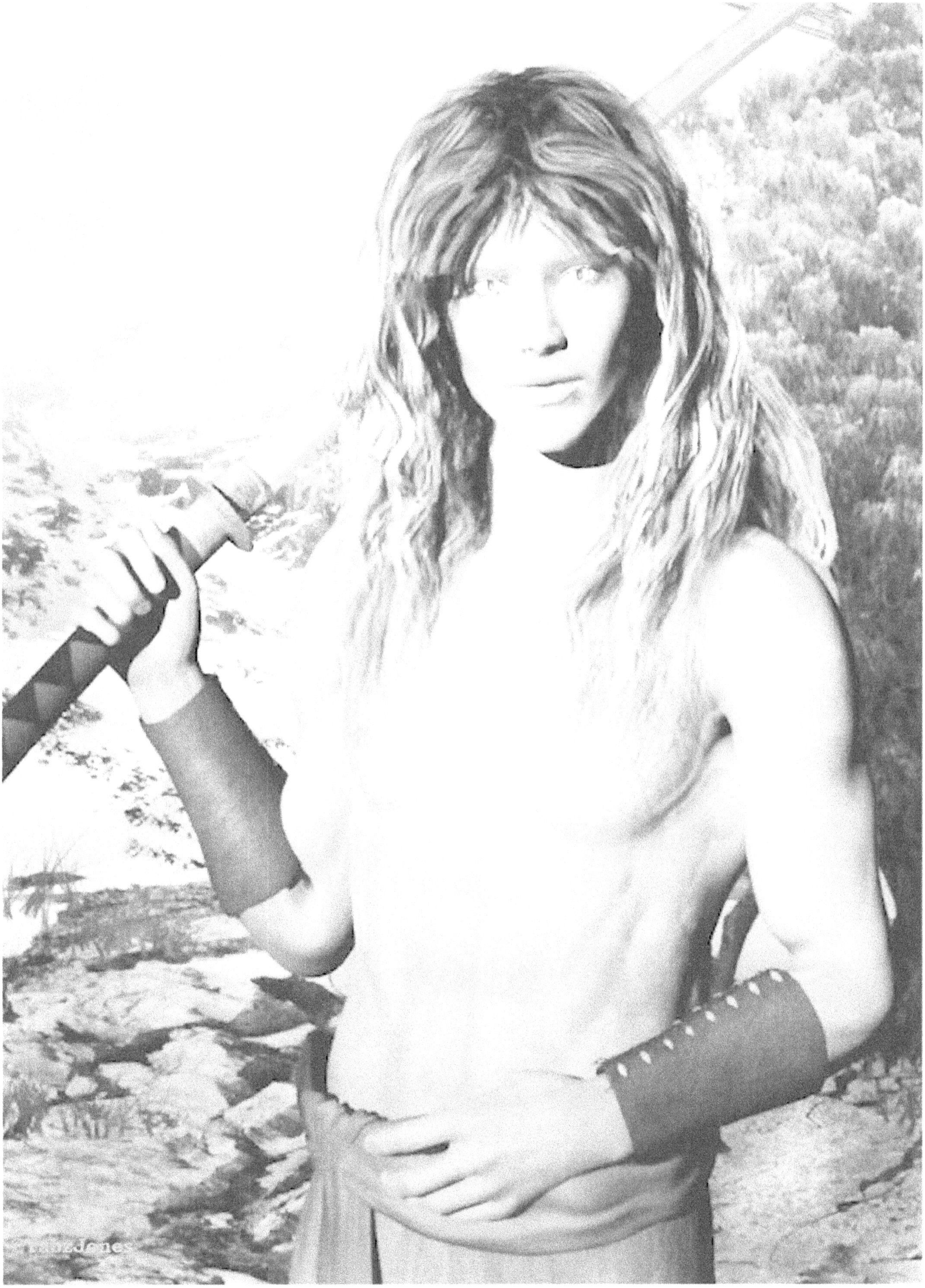

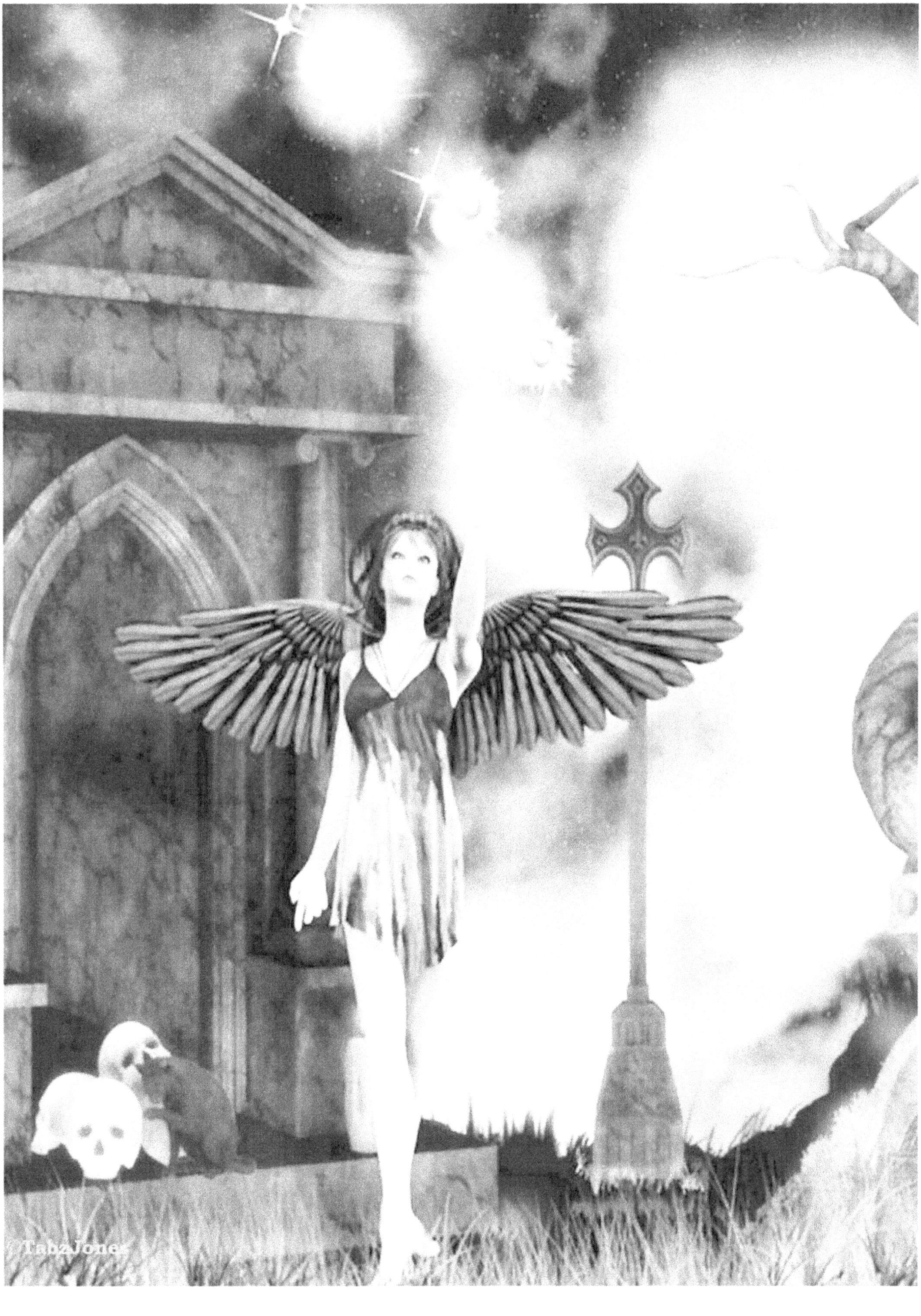
TabzJones

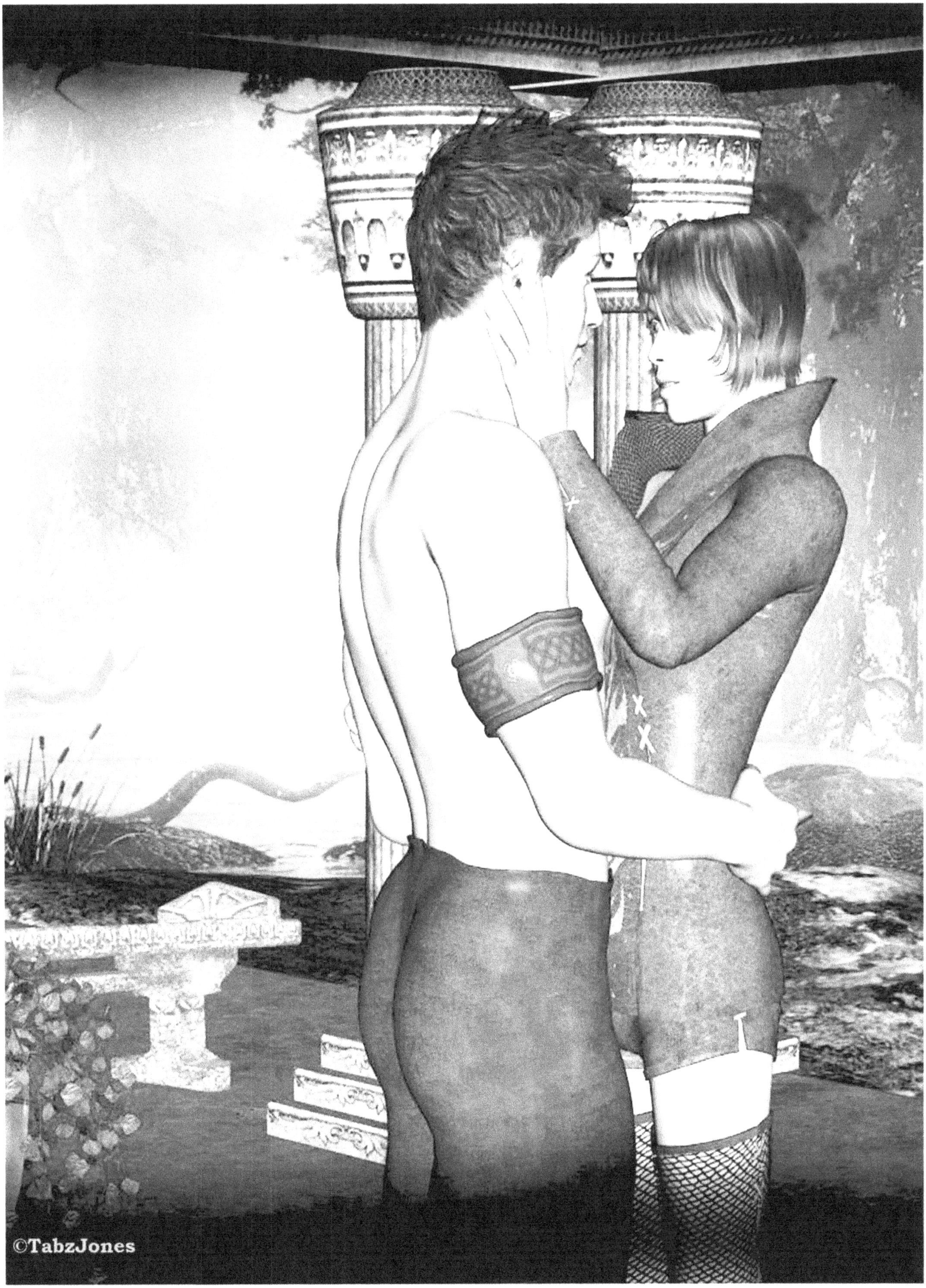
©TabzJones

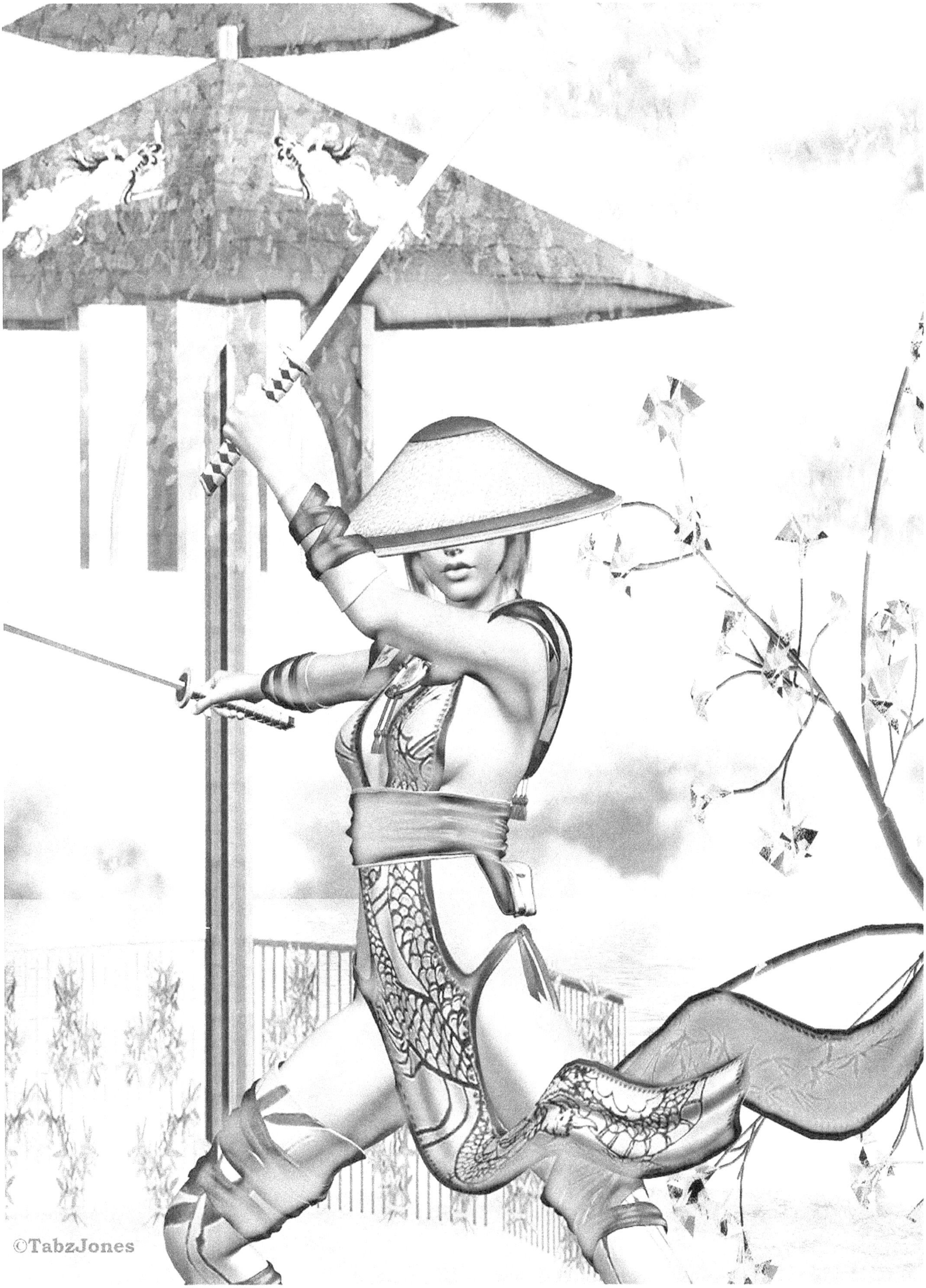
©TabzJones

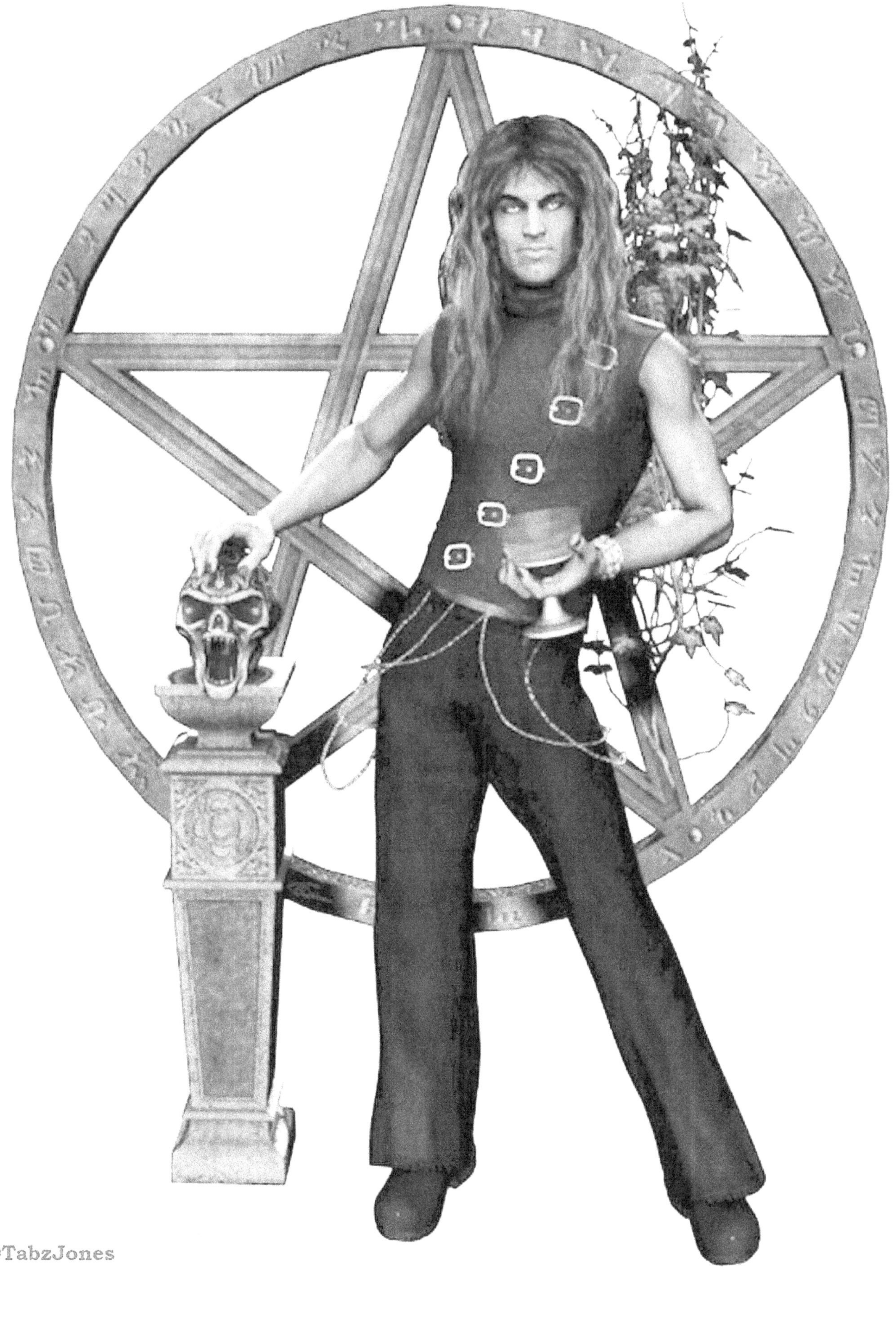

www.ingramcontent.com/pod-product-compliance
Lightning Source LLC
Chambersburg PA
CBHW081608200526
45169CB00021B/2464
9781530376070